How to Live Confidently
in a Hostile World

ALSO BY JAMES S. HEWETT

Books:
Illustrations Unlimited

Periodicals (Editor):
Parables, Etc.
The Pastor's Story File
Locus Classicus

JAMES HEWETT

How to Live Confidently in a Hostile World

WORD PUBLISHING
Dallas · London · Sydney · Singapore

Unless otherwise indicated, Scripture quotations in this book
are from the Revised Standard Version of the Bible (RSV),
copyrighted 1946, 1952, © 1971, 1973 by the
Division of Christian Education of the National Council
of the Churches of Christ in the U.S.A., and are used by permission.

Other Scripture quotations are from the following sources:

The King James Version of the Bible (KJV).

The Holy Bible, New International Version (NIV).
Copyright © 1973, 1978, 1984 International Bible Society.
Used by permission of Zondervan Bible Publishers.

The New American Standard Bible (NASB), © The Lockman Foundation
1960, 1962, 1963, 1968, 1971, 1972, 1973, 1975, 1977.

The New Testament in Modern English (PHILLIPS)
by J. B. Phillips, published by The Macmillan Company,
© 1958, 1960, 1972 by J. B. Phillips.

The Living Bible (LB), copyright 1971
by Tyndale House Publishers, Wheaton, IL. Used by permission.

Library of Congress Cataloging-in-Publication Data:

Hewett, James S., 1930–
   How to live confidently in a hostile world / James S. Hewett.
   p. cm.
   ISBN 0-8499-3122-3
   1. Success—Religious aspects—Christianity. 2. Attitude
(Psychology)—Religious aspects—Christianity. 3. Self-realization—
Religious aspects—Christianity. I. Title.
BV4598.3H49 1989
248.4—dc19   88-374-1
                                                       CIP

Printed in the United States of America

9801239 AGF 0987654321

Dedicated to Ken Johnson,
unique and gifted friend who has gone ahead

Contents

Catch the *1*
Super Wave to Freedom

Papillon is the story of a brilliant escape from an "escape proof" island prison. Some years back this riveting tale was the subject of a bestselling book and a movie starring Steve McQueen. One of the great adventures of our day, it is the first-person story of Henri Charrière, known as Papillon, "The Butterfly," because of a butterfly tattoo on his chest.

During the 1930s, Papillon was unjustly condemned to the French Penal Colony on the Îles du Salut just off the coast of French Guiana. After eight years in solitary confinement and eight escape attempts, Papillon was finally taken to the infamous Devil's Island—the same island that had been the scene of Captain Alfred Dreyfus's lonely four-year exile near the turn of the century.

Everyone *knew* it was impossible to escape from Devil's Island. In fact, few guards were needed there because the waves pounded so treacherously along the rugged coastline. Anyone who attempted escape would be instantly and mercilessly hurled back against the rocks and never live to tell the story.

But Papillon *did* escape from Devil's Island because, after five long years of imprisonment, he made an important discovery. He learned one of the basic secrets of life—that the very forces that some men see as imprisoning could also be seen as a highway to freedom. Papillon escaped because he saw opportunity where others only saw restraint. This is how it happened. . . .

═══ THE HIGH DRAMA OF ESCAPE ═══

When Papillon first arrived on the island, he vowed to "forget about the dying and concentrate exclusively on winning and being free." Where other prisoners on the "escape-proof" island accepted their situation as hopeless, Papillon would not give in to such thoughts. Instead, he focused specifically and singularly upon escape, and it was this focus that eventually showed him the means of escape.

Papillon made his discovery as he patiently observed the surf pounding over the craggy coastline of the island. There was one place along the cliffs where the tons of wave-power broke ferociously into a horseshoe-shaped inlet. By experimentation, he found that every seventh wave in this inlet was a "super" wave that approached as straight as a cannonball with its own unique thunderous roar and crashed so hard against the cove that the returning waters worked their way back out to sea with a "wild, churning . . . making a rumble like a hundred wagon loads of stones being dumped."

Papillon named this recurring, powerful seventh wave "Lisette," and he learned through experimentation that this particular wave pattern could be used to carry large bags of coconuts far enough out to sea so they would not be hurled back onto shore. When Lisette arrived, she dragged everything caught in her churning foam back to sea. And Lisette came with a special extraordinary force at high tide.

Once he had discovered Lisette's powerful secret, Papillon set out to study the waves, the currents, the tides, and the phases of the moon. Through his computations he figured that at high tide a one hundred fifty-five-pound man on a coconut-bag raft would be carried by the super wave Lisette far up the coastline to Grande Terre and to freedom. And he resolved to make use of Lisette to help him escape.

He called upon two fellow prisoners to help him—Chang, a Chinese man he had known well (imprisoned for piracy and murder), and Silvain, an athletic man over six feet tall and all muscle. Though Chang was willing to help with the preparations, he was not willing to actually join their attempt at escape. Silvain took a week to be convinced and then threw in his lot with Papillon. The plans were drawn in detail for the great day. Papillon tells the story:

> It was all set for Sunday at ten in the evening. There would be a full moon, hence a twenty-five-foot tide and Lisette . . . would be at full strength.
>
> I would sleep all of Saturday and Sunday. Departure at ten—the tide would have started to ebb two hours before. . . .

And so the preparations were made and they waited on the top of the cliff for Lisette, the giant wave, to come.

> She was on her way; Lisette was coming straight for us, standing up like the spire of a church. With her usual deafening roar she broke over our rocks and swept toward the cliff.
>
> I threw myself in a fraction of a second before my buddy, but we were close together as Lisette sucked us out into the open sea with dizzying speed. In less than five minutes we were over three hundred yards from shore. . . . Chang had scampered up to Dreyfus' bench and, holding a white rag in his hand, was waving a last good-bye. Now we were a good five minutes beyond the dangerous area where the waves heading for Diable [Devil's Island] formed.
>
> * * *
>
> The night went smoothly. Then we felt a powerful change in the direction of the sea. The tide which had drawn us out had turned and was now pushing us toward Grande Terre.*

What a moment—the inexorable tide pushing Papillon to Grande Terre—and to freedom! The very force of nature that other prisoners saw only as a prison, Papillon saw as an express train to a new life full of the riches of freedom. This man who forgot about dying and concentrated exclusively on winning harnessed that force of nature and rode it to freedom.

═══ THE PURPOSE OF THIS BOOK ═══

This book is about catching the super waves that lead to fulfillment and freedom, about living confidently and fully in a world that can be threatening and hostile as well as beautiful and exciting.

There are God-given principles that can liberate you as you learn to go with the forces of life. You can gain insight into the dynamics of God's creation that can bring you a life enriched with the fulfillment of your deepest heart desires. Even if you have felt like a chronic prisoner and victim in life, you can be transformed into a confident winner. And the really good news is that you can do it without becoming hostile and crabby yourself!

Are you a victim or a victor? Are you in charge of your life and making things happen? Are you an initiator or simply a reactor? Are you the sort that is intimidated and pummelled by hostile

*Henri Charrière, *Papillon,* tr. June P. Wilson and Walter B. Michaels (New York: Pocket Books, 1971), pp. 386–389.

forces that have left you unfulfilled and impoverished? Or are you ready to discover the God-given principles—the Lisettes and her sisters—that can carry you to a more abundant life, that can give you a more confident attitude toward life?

=== LOSERS INTO WINNERS ===

This book is designed to help uptight losers like Charles Schultz's Charlie Brown become likable winners. It is set up to help people who are always thinking they could get ahead if they could "only get organized" or focused. It is designed to help people who have given up on being successful because they really want to be nice people and they've bought the lie that "nice guys always finish last."

The truth is that *anybody* can be a winner in life because there are many super waves built into the universe—many ways of becoming the kind of person with a lifestyle that wins. You don't have to be a super salesman or a top-flight executive to be a success—perhaps you will end up as a happy free-lance artist or a confident homemaker or a fulfilled social worker. But whatever your hopes and dreams, forces are available that can move you toward a rewarding life—in which you are a healthier, wealthier, and a wiser person because you understand and are harnessing God's built-in powerful principles.

The universe has always contained these principles that can help you set yourself up for real success—the kind of success that truly matters . . . and lasts. Don't waste your time or energy any longer in being a victim—of someone else or of your own limited vision. Begin the life of a conqueror. Learn about life's opportunities and seize them. Jesus said, "I am come that you might have life and have it more abundantly" (John 10:11). Learn what you need to do to enjoy that abundant life that is waiting for you. In the words of Samuel Johnson, "To improve the golden moment of opportunity, and catch the good that is within our reach, is the great art of life."

Remember reading those grand old seafaring tales like *Moby Dick* and *Two Years Before the Mast*? The skippers waited until high tide and left port on the moving of the tide—they harnessed the forces of nature to work for them. They wouldn't waste their energy by setting to sea against an incoming tide.

And yet, strangely enough, many people live their lives always going, as it were, upstream and against the tide—always somehow out of phase, out of sync, with the currents of reality.

Why labor against the tide when a mere adjustment in schedule would make the tide your ally? Losers in life attempt to accomplish things while pitting themselves against reality and then wonder why it doesn't work.

You can make these powerful forces your servants—or you can fight them as hostile opponents and try to go against life's grain. Just as there are laws of gravity, meteorology, heat transfer, and fluid mechanics; so there are behavioral, attitudinal, and spiritual principles that can bring your life more enrichment, prosperity, satisfaction, health, serenity, purpose and accomplishment.

=== JOIN THE GROUP ===

The amazing thing is that so few have truly mastered these principles. Too many people struggle on in their frustration—defeated, settling for misery or dull dissatisfaction when they could join the circle of those who regularly ride the super waves to freedom. In this book you will have the opportunity to study and master these super-wave principles for your life's enrichment. You will learn to:

- CLARIFY your deepest and truest aspirations that when satisfied can bring you the fulfillment you seek.
- UNDERSTAND the importance and techniques of purging your life of the energy-draining demands of others.
- FOCUS your energies so as to move effectively toward your personal goals.
- MASTER the keys of self-motivation to do the things you really want to do.

These principles are not new. They were known to men like Abraham, Moses, and King David. They have been used also by men of our century—Thomas Edison, Albert Einstein, Andrew Carnegie, Leo Tolstoy, O.J. Simpson, Fran Tarkenton, Og Mandino, John Ralston, and many others.

These are tools that have helped people do things that others couldn't. Such tools give a person a big advantage—as big as the advantage a shovel gives over using your hands to dig or the advantage a lever gives over using brute force to lift a weight. And these tools aren't hidden; they are lying around waiting to be claimed and put to use! To find and use them is to make your life more confident and fulfilling.

═══ *SEIZING OPPORTUNITIES* ═══

In Act IV of Shakespeare's *Julius Caesar*, Brutus and Cassius are debating what to do in the face of the oncoming armies of Octavian and Antony. As they confer in their tent outside Sardis, they argue as to the best course of action—whether they should wait and fight Antony near Sardis after he advanced to them or take the initiative and advance on Antony near the Plains of Philippi in Macedonia. Brutus says:

> There is a tide in the affairs of men
> Which, taken at the flood, leads on to fortune;
> Omitted, all voyage of their life
> Is bound in shallows and in miseries.
> On such a full sea are we now afloat,
> And we must take the current when it serves
> Or lose our ventures.
>
> *Julius Caesar*, act 4, scene 3

Here is one of life's potent truths—one of the keys that unlocks the path of success: the moments of opportunity must be recognized and seized. Or, as Maltbie Babcock put it, "Opportunities do not come with their values stamped upon them. Everyone must be challenged. A day dawns, quite like other days; in it a single hour comes, quite like others; but in that day and in that hour the chance of a lifetime faces us. To face every opportunity of life thoughtfully and ask its meaning bravely and earnestly, is the only way to meet the supreme opportunities when they come, whether open-faced or disguised."

Where are the hidden opportunities in your life? As you read this book and do the exercises you can discover opportunities that may be invisible to others around you, just as Papillon saw coconuts as a life raft and Lisette, the super wave, as a railroad to freedom. You can begin to prepare your own custom-made raft for the incoming wave that will sweep you powerfully into a more satisfying life.

═══ *EASY OR HARD?* ═══

Is it easy or hard? It is both!

It is easy in that the rules are so simple that a child can understand them (and many children learn them early, almost instinctively). At times you will say—"Oh, it can't be that simple!"

And that is where the difficulty comes in—for it sometimes seems too hard to do the simple and obvious things that *must* be done.

Papillon and his friend were easily swept out to sea—all they did was jump off the cliff with their coconuts at the right time. Such jumping is not physically hard. But it takes planning and preparation to be ready to jump at the right time—to "not only strike while the iron is hot but make it hot by striking." And it takes courage to jump, to commit yourself to the current that leads to freedom.

It is hard to make that final decision to jump. It was too hard for Papillon's friend Chang, so he stayed behind and waved his handkerchief as Papillon was swept away to freedom and a new life.

═══ TOO LATE? ═══

You may be thinking, *All this is fine for younger people just starting out in life, but it's too late for me. I'm too old* (or *I have a family to support,* or *I've gone too far down another road*).

Is it too late for you to begin to find your fulfillment? No!

I recently learned of an 82-year-old Black man named George Lockland who earned his Master's degree after receiving his B.A. two years before. And the truly exciting part of his story is that, as soon as he finished his degrees, he immediately set out to find the right kind of job where he could use his new skills.

Shortly after the release of James Michener's *Alaska,* I received a descriptive flyer from the Book of the Month Club advertising the book as that month's Main Selection. The flyer contained a short article by Michener entitled, "Why Alaska?" in which he told that he had been thinking about writing a novel about Alaska since 1947:

> Why did I not start researching and writing at that time? The explanation seems ridiculous, but at age 40, I was afraid I might be too old to withstand the rigors of an Alaskan winter, which hovers at 50 degrees below zero along the Yukon River. So in obedience to a rule I've set for myself, never to write about a place in which I haven't lived, I shied away from the Alaska opportunity, though I knew I should tackle that powerful terrain where the United States and the Soviet Union stand toe-to-toe across the Bering Sea.
>
> The long years 1947–1984 passed with my often thinking of trying my luck in Alaska and always drawing back with apprehension: "I'm too old." Then irrationally, after a major heart attack and a

quintuple bypass and just before my 80th birthday, I thought . . .
"If I'm ever going to do that Alaska book, let's do it now while I have
the energy." Without any further speculation or hesitance I moved
to Alaska, set up my typewriter in a log cabin on the campus of
Sheldon Jackson Junior College in Sitka and proceeded to dig into
every cranny of Alaskan life.

I spent one Christmas at Fort Yukon just over the Arctic Circle
and a week in Eagle with the thermometer at minus 52. I visited
Prudhoe Bay, on the edge of the Arctic Ocean, twice, and Barrow,
where the Eskimos go for whales, three times. And I took a splendid cruise through all the islands of the Aleutian archipelago, landing on some eight of them, always wading the last 50 yards to shore
in hip boots.

I studied the salmon industry and explored the great glaciers,
and I made friends at an Eskimo school far above the Arctic Circle,
where in January and much of February the nights are 24 hours
long, and in June and July the days never end. My experiences so
delighted me that I wondered, "Why didn't I do this 40 years ago?"*

No, it's not too late until you've given up and decided it's too
late.

OTHERS HAVE GONE BEFORE US

Now, when we speak of harnessing the forces of nature, we need
not enter life like a sailor taking to uncharted waters. We need not,
like Papillon, look to the billowing winds and currents of life as if
they were unknown and unfathomed. To put it another way, we do
not have to reinvent the wheel; it has been done!

Many have made the journey before us and have charted the way.
The sacred Scriptures underline and clarify the principles for success. People of wisdom and understanding in virtually every civilization and culture have found these keys and passed them on. We
only need to follow their example.

Remember, God built these principles into his universe because he wants us to achieve and accomplish good and satisfying
things. He wants us to concentrate on being his free children.

THE DIVIDING LINE

Here stands one of the continental divides that separates people—
a dividing line that separates the winners from those who persist

*Book of the Month Club News, July 1988.

in losing. On one side of the line are those who observe carefully and have the courage to use the forces God has put in nature and placed at our disposal. On the other side are the timorous who hold back and remain prisoners resigned to their fears and their doubts, captives to their frustrations and impotence.

Are you willing to sit fearfully in the backwash of life and let the waves buffet you? Are you pummelled and crushed by the seemingly hostile forces of nature? Or are you willing to climb the cliff, build your coconuts raft, see where the tides are running that push men to success—and leap to freedom? As industrialist Roy Chapin has written, "The best men are not those who have waited for chances, but who have taken them—besieged the chance, conquered the chance and made the chance their servitor."

=== SUMMARY ===

Papillon dedicated himself to escape, observed the forces around him, and seized the moment to ride those forces to freedom. Losers can become winners when they join those who understand and go with the currents of nature—basic principles built into the universe. It is both easy and hard. These are simple rules that are available to all but take courage and perseverance to apply. When you ride the super wave to freedom—you become more confident and successful in almost every dimension of life.

Successful Winners 2

What do you truly believe God had in mind when he designed you? Do you think he expected you to be an assembly-line, mediocre, crabby, impoverished loser? I don't believe it!

The Bible teaches that God has good plans for us. He wants us to experience his best intentions. God's plan is not some darkly kept secret hidden away in the bowels of the earth. He has made it plain—what he wants for us is life abundant! As God told the children of Israel, "For I know the plans I have for you, says the Lord, plans for welfare and not for evil, to give you a future and a hope" (Jer. 29:11).

I believe that God intends for each one of us to be a uniquely prosperous and confident winner who succeeds in life. But the problem that confronts us here is the rich and varied meanings of words like *success* and *winning*. They mean different things to different people.

WHAT IS SUCCESS?

Phil's idea of success was sexual conquest. Years ago Phil and I worked together at the old Olympic Garage (now torn down) across the street from the YWCA in Seattle. For him, life revolved around picking up girls from the Y, "making it" with them sexually, and keeping his wife from finding out.

Floyd had a different idea of success; he spent most of his discretionary hours planning for the day he could become a professional tennis player. He earned a more than adequate living as an electrical engineer, but he dreamed of the day he could quit engineering and hit the courts as a pro.

Bob, my sales manager the summer that I sold the Audio Bible to help pay for seminary, was a spellbinder of a salesman. My own sales career came to quick end because I didn't really believe in the necessity or the high quality of a product line—the Bible on phonograph records. But Bob had dreams of selling a set of the Audio Bible to virtually every family in Southern California. For him, success was calibrated in number of sales and total of dollars. He was as assertive as a Mack truck (and about as delicate).

Sally is a widow. Her friends think she is one of the most accomplished and all-around wonderful people to walk on this earth. But she won't feel really successful until she goes back to school to finish up her college work.

For John success means academic honors; for Art it is helping his grown kids to get out on their own. For Stella it means being able to retire early; for Robin it is the expansion of her business. For Ken it means becoming president of the company; for Karen it means raising healthy, happy kids.

We could go on. Everyone has a different idea of what success means for him or her.

Even if we define success simply as "achieving a goal," we are left with the fact that both the goals themselves and what it means to achieve them are different for different people. For many, simply the sense of inner satisfaction, of being in a process of growth is sufficient to spell success, whether or not one ever "arrives." Other people can't feel satisfied unless they reach measurable standards they have set for themselves. Goals have less to do with external standards imposed by society, more to do with one's own inner desires. In many cases they involve a desire to strengthen one's spiritual roots.

Over the last few decades the popular definitions of success have undergone a good deal of scrutiny and reassessment. As Walden Howard reported in the June 1974 issue of *Faith At Work* magazine, in the early days of our nation a popular, materialistic "rags to riches" notion was fairly widespread. But gradually the idea of success began to include "quality of life" issues that could not always be measured in terms of wealth or power.

This is shown clearly in the results of a study done by the American Management Association in the early 1970s. This study showed that 70 percent of the respondents were unhappy in what they were doing and would like to make a change. Half had already changed their line of work. More than half faced pressures to conform to standards which make them uncomfortable.

Almost one-third felt that job requirements had adversely affected their health. And most of them had come to a new definition of success, one that had less to do with material well-being and more to do with, as Howard put it, "the richness of human experience and opportunity for true self-expression."

My own counseling with Yuppies and the Baby Boom generation suggests that many of them have a difficult time coming to terms with a clear definition of success. (Just watch the television show *Thirtysomething* and watch their struggle!)

But even though the specifics of success are hard to pin down, it is possible to isolate some common elements that apply to all success—whether it is that of a Ghandi or Thoreau or the more capitalistic success of an Andrew Carnegie. Howard Whitman, in his book *Success Is Within You,* suggests five of these:

- Success must include an abiding sense of PURPOSE.
- Success does not mean always winning, but having a GOOD BATTING AVERAGE. There will almost always be some failures along the way.
- Success has a PRICE TAG—it is not free.
- Success must include a sense of PERSONAL SATISFACTION —it must be enjoyed.
- Success must have a SPIRITUAL element—a feeling of being related somehow to the greater purposes of life and the Author of those purposes. To be truly successful is to be in tune with God.

These five elements point toward a definition of success that is both useful and universal: *Success is living your life in such a way that you are in the continual process of discovering the gifts and authentic God-given potential that is yours, developing goals that are consistent with those discoveries, and moving steadily toward meeting those goals.* The goals must be consistent with your authentic God-given identity, and they must be realistically planned for and reached as a lifelong process. As someone has said, "Success isn't a harbor, it's a lifelong journey."

Psychologist Abraham Maslow used the term *self-authenticating* to describe a person who is successful according to the above definition. I believe the self becomes authentic only when it is living in harmony with the unique way God crafted it.

It is the thesis of this book that God has provided super waves— "Lisettes"—that are available even within the seemingly chaotic and hostile world and that we can harness to reach the specific kind of healthy success we have defined for ourselves. For Papillon, it meant escape and freedom, and the place to latch onto it was in the foment of the pounding surf. Unless you, too, are being held prisoner on an island, success will mean something different for you.

=== A WINNING MIND ===

In recent years there has been a great deal written about winning and losing. I like the definition of winning by James and Jongeward:

> The words *winner* and *loser* have many meanings—each human being is born as something new, something that never existed before, he is born with what he needs to win at life. Each person in his own way can see, hear, touch, taste and think for himself. Each can be a significant, thinking, aware and creatively productive person in his own right. A winner! When we refer to a person as a winner, we do not mean one who beats the other guy by winning over him and making him lose. To us a winner is one who responds authentically by being credible, trustworthy, responsible and genuine, both as an individual and as a member of society. A loser is one who fails to respond authentically.*

To an important extent, whether we are a winner or a loser is a matter of how we see ourselves—particularly in relationship to the setbacks of life—the mistakes we make and how we interpret them.

Charlie Brown in the "Peanuts" comic strip is a perfect example of a "loser" mentality. In one strip, for example, Charlie Brown is playing hockey. He's the goalie. Pigpen takes a swat at the puck and zips it right between Charlie Brown's legs for a score. Charlie Brown's teammates are all over him for allowing the score. They throw him out of the game. He leaves muttering to himself, "Rats! I can't do anything right. I can't play hockey, I can't play checkers, I can't fly kites, I can't do anything right."

And then Lucy comes along. She says, "What's the matter, Charlie Brown?"

"I don't know. I'm depressed. I don't feel good. I think maybe I'm coming down with the Asian flu."

*Muriel James and Dorothy Jongeward, *Born To Win* (New York: Signet/New American Library, 1978), pp. 1–2.

"The Asian flu? That's been over for six months," Lucy says. She leaves laughing to herself. "What a guy! Everybody else got the Asian flu six months ago, and he's just now getting it."

In the last frame Charlie Brown is shown sitting alone and disconsolate, muttering to himself, "Good grief. I can't even get sick right!"

Too many people carry around this kind of "I just can't get it right" mindset. But living a confident life in a hostile world means knowing and reminding yourself that you were both created and redeemed to be an authentic winner.

In Genesis we read,

> Then God said, "Let us make man *in our image*, after our likeness; and let them have dominion over the fish of the sea, and over the birds of the air, and over the cattle, and over the earth, and over every creeping thing that creeps upon the earth."

And then the account continues,

> So God created man in his own image . . . male and female he created them. . . . And it was so. And God saw everything that he had made, and behold, it was *very good* (1:27, 30–31, emphasis added).

What a winning start this is—made in God's image, given global dominion, and formally and enthusiastically pronounced "Good" by the Creator!

Martin Buber tells the story of an old Rabbi who, on his deathbed, saw himself as a loser. He lamented that in the world to come he would not be asked why he wasn't Moses but rather he would be asked why he wasn't himself.

God created within you as a uniquely worthwhile individual—a discrete entity in life. You don't have to be Moses to be a winner. You have to be *you!*—the authentic *YOU* God had in mind.

WINNING MINDS FROM CREATION

We are created in God's image. Therefore we have minds, even as God is the ground and source of infinite mind. There are obvious differences, of course. God's thought is infinite and ours finite. A fascinating insight is found in Ecclesiastes 3, which says God made "everything beautiful in its time; also he has put eternity into man's mind, yet so that he cannot find out what God has done from the beginning to the end" (v. 11). God has planted eternity in our minds, and yet has limited us.

Do you have a winning mind? And what does that mean? Is your mind growing and functioning the way that God designed it?

Or did you reach a plateau in the eighth grade and say, "Well, that's about as far as it goes, Charlie. Turn off the switches; we'll coast from here to the grave"?

I hope not. You have an alive mind designed for searching, inquiring, looking, weighing, learning, and discovering. These processes are like super waves for your mind's successful growth. Give yourself to lifelong learning of eternal truth.

WINNING MINDS FROM REDEMPTION

God wants your mind to win even in the midst of a fallen and hostile world, and he has a plan by which he does it. He *renews* the mind as it is filled with his knowledge and his presence.

As Paul writes in Romans 12:1–2:

> I appeal to you therefore, brethren, by the mercies of God, to present your bodies as a living sacrifice, holy and acceptable to God, which is your spiritual worship. Do not be conformed to this world but be *transformed by the renewal of your mind*, that you may prove what is the will of God, what is good and acceptable and perfect.

Consider that! Proving—demonstrating the validity of—the will of God by your mind.

So often when you hear people talking about discerning God's will, they will speak of it almost as something "way out there"—something different or foreign or strange that they've got to search out and discover like a needle in a haystack. (And then, they suspect, it probably will pointedly and uncomfortably impinge itself upon their lives.) It's as if God's got one idea (well-concealed) and we've most likely got a completely different idea, and we've got to really hustle to figure out what God's is.

But Paul suggests in Romans 12 that we have the ability to "prove" what the will of God is for us because we have been *transformed* and our minds have been *renewed*. That's kind of mind-boggling in itself. And in 1 Corinthians 2:14–16, Paul elaborates on this idea by contrasting "spiritual" and "unspiritual" persons:

> The unspiritual man does not receive the gifts of the Spirit of God, for they are folly to him, and he is not able to understand

them because they are spiritually discerned. [He just doesn't have the equipment to handle it.] The spiritual man judges all things, but is himself to be judged by no one. For who has known the mind of the Lord so as to instruct him? But we have the mind of Christ.

We have the mind of Christ! Paul was not saying, "Oh Lord, I am stupid, an ignoramus. I know nothing; show me what you want. I'm so dense." No! God gave him a mind; and God transformed that mind with the presence of Christ in it; and Paul proved, by and through life's experiences, what the will of God was.

Even though he readily admitted he was the chief of sinners and that he lived as the frequent butt of a hostile world's persecutions (2 Cor. 11:16–33), Paul knew he was a winner because he understood clearly the mind that God had built within him. And he made sure it was focused and tuned in such a way that it was susceptible to the incredible truths of God.

There is a parallel passage in Colossians 3:9–10: "Do not lie to one another, seeing that you have put off the old nature with its practices." Paul is talking about the process of regeneration—putting off the old nature. Then Paul continues, "put on the new nature, which is being renewed in knowledge after the image of its creator."

It all started with creation—God gave us a fantastic winning mind at creation that got a bit screwed up through the Fall. As the theologians put it, in the Fall the image of God was sullied, but not utterly destroyed. Though damaged, there is still a point of contact, a light within each person (John 1:9). And, through regeneration in Christ, our minds can be renewed, brought back closer to a godly image again and be restored as winning minds. There's a new mind available to you, and it is the regenerating mind of Christ.

Proverbs 22:17 says, "Apply your mind to my knowledge." Some people seem to think that Christians should somehow have to check their brains at the door of the church. We talk about childlike faith, and that's valid. But *childlike* faith doesn't necessarily mean a *childish* mind. God has given us minds to use, to grow, to think with, to mature—and these minds are instruments of God.

Think of this—your mind was fashioned as a unique receptacle of the mind of God. And unless the mind of his Son, Jesus Christ, is resident in your mind, it is not growing and expressing itself the way it was designed to be.

Very often we think of Christ dwelling in our hearts, but Christ dwells in the mind as well. Do you have the mind that is thinking about the knowledge of God? Your mind was designed to know God. Your mind was designed to know and experience the reality of God, the values of God. What is your mind filled with? What is it occupied with? Is your mind growing and expanding?

As a former colleague, Clair Morrow, used to say, "God gave you two ends to use, one to think with and one to sit on. Heads you win, tails you lose!"

═══ WINNING CHOICES ═══

God wants us to make winning choices. God didn't make us robots and say, "I have tested plan #863, which I want everybody to use. Here is a whole series of hoops—now you go and jump through them!" In effect, God said he was going to give each of us the opportunity to make a series of choices as to how we want to glorify him, how we want to live out that rich potential he has given us.

Shortly before his death, Moses shared God's message with the children of Israel: "I've set before you life and death. I've shown you that if you go *this* way, you will have trouble, but that if you go *that* way, you will have a rich, prosperous life. Now you choose! Choose the kind of life you want!" (Deut. 30:19, my paraphrase).

Joshua presented the same kind of choices to the children of Israel: "Choose this day whom you will serve. . . . as for me and my house, we will serve the Lord" (Josh. 24:15).

In both the Old and New Testaments, we see that God gives us choices. He also gives us laws and instructions: "Look, this is the way it all works; now you can choose to go with it or fight it."

There are powerful forces in life you can chose to ride as super waves, Lisettes. Or you can simply be pummelled by those forces if you do not understand them.

One of the first controversies in the early church involved the observance of ceremonial days. Some of the people who had been raised in Judaism wanted to observe the Sabbaths and other holy days, while others felt that the Jewish customs needed to be left behind.

Paul, writing in response to this controversy, doesn't say, "Look, here's the way everybody has got to do it." No! He says, "One man esteems one day as better than another, while another esteems all days alike. Let everyone be fully convinced in his own mind" (Rom. 14:5). In other words, *"YOU* decide how you want to work it out."

In 2 Corinthians 9:6–7, the issue is stewardship and generosity. Paul doesn't say, "Here's the law: Everybody gives 10.6 percent of the gross income, and then you deduct this, etc." No! Paul says, in effect, "Here's a principle: Give a lot, and you're going to get back a lot; be a cheapskate, and you are not going to get much back. Each person must do as he has made up his mind."

There are choices for all of us to make. God has given you a variety of options as to the quality and character of your life as well as the "how-to's" of doing certain things.

Are you making winning choices? To some, freedom is a burden; political leaders down through the centuries have made use of that fact and taken away people's freedom in return for bread. This ploy has been used by dictators from Caesar to Hitler.

Another "Peanuts" strip: One semester poor Linus doesn't make the honor roll. He tells Charlie Brown, "Everyone is so upset because I didn't make the honor roll. My mother is upset, my father's upset, my teacher's upset, the principal's upset. Good grief! They all say the same thing—they're disappointed because I have such potential." Linus cries out in the last frame, "There's no heavier burden than a great potential."

Perhaps that is the kind of burden you feel. Maybe you don't want to have a great potential or great opportunity. But God has given you the choice of what you will do with your life. The kind of choices you make should be winning choices—choices that are the accepted responsibility of a person who rejoices in the freedom God gives!

═══ INGREDIENTS IN WINNING CHOICES ═══

A winning choice has two key elements: it is *informed* and it is *authentic*.

INFORMED CHOICES

An informed choice is one that's based upon knowledge of reality —knowledge of God's Word and how the world actually works. Winning choices are not made against reality; you only lose if you make choices based on anything other than truth. (Just as you can't play chess if you don't know, or you ignore, the unique possible moves of the knight.)

Be informed in making your choices. Be informed by the physical and spiritual realities that operate in our world and then gladly and joyfully make your choices.

Papillon made a choice to leap to freedom—but it was not without careful study of the currents, the wave patterns, the tides, and the physical configuration of the cove—plus a good deal of experimentation with bags of coconuts. His choice was neither rash nor premature; it was well informed.

AUTHENTIC CHOICES

Winning choices are authentic. That is, they grow out of our own value system and are not swayed by false values or other people's values. One of the most pervasive problems we face in our day is that many people spend their time (and make their choice) trying to live up to the expectations of others—expectations that may not be valid for them.

"Peanuts" again: Charlie Brown, looking out the window, says to his sister, "Gee, I'm glad it's raining today. Now I can stay inside and read." She comes over to him and says, "Well, couldn't you stay inside and read if it wasn't raining?" He answers, "Oh! Whenever the sun is shining I feel obligated to play outside."

That's the way many of us go through life. Somebody has dumped on us all kinds of obligations to carry out life in certain ways. We can't make authentic choices with that kind of intimidation bearing down on us.

══ WINNING EMOTIONS ══

God has revealed himself to be a feeling, affectionate being, and he has given us an affective dimension as well. He wants us to be winners emotionally—in our feelings as well as in our minds and choices.

Our feelings are powerful and insistent, and they are also important. They assist us in a life that is rich and healthy and growing. And they can be important clues to inner realities.

But because feelings are so powerful, they can push us in wrong directions—because they are not always reliable as the basis for our choices. I can feel I want certain things that are not wise or good for me. I can see a beautiful girl and feel single—but I'm not single! Or I can feel angry with my co-workers when they are really not the cause of my problem.

Sometimes feelings need to be changed, overridden, or ignored as invalid, impractical, or unfeasible. The counselor who is attracted to the person he is counseling needs to consider some of his sexual feelings as non-operative, just as the obese person needs to treat his lust for coconut cream pie as an unhealthy aberration. An angry person needs to choose not to take her anger out on innocent bystanders, and someone who feels worthless needs to find ways to remind himself of how much God values him.

The Scriptures speak frequently about the heart as a center of emotions. When the feeling life is messed up, one is really wretched. "The heart is deceitful above all things, and desperately corrupt" according to Jeremiah 17:9. On the other hand, when the affections are healthy and winning and growing the way God designed them to grow, they are pure, creating a "clean heart" in us (Ps. 51:10).

SOURCES OF WINNING EMOTIONS

Love of God and Neighbor. Winning feelings—healthy emotions —how do we get them? First, we need to understand that Christ's *agape* love—that strength or ability to reach out unselfishly and care for others—is the source of a healthy emotional life. Jesus said to love both God and neighbor "because [God] first loved us" (1 John 4:19).

Victor Frankl has defined love as "the desire to realize the potential that is in another." I like that. Love is a deep concern to help another person bring to flower the very best that is in him or her. It is a benevolent concern for the best interests of another.

When we love one another within the community of God's family, we are able to relate to one another in ways of genuine mutuality. When Paul talks about "edifying the body of Christ, the church" he is talking about this kind of thing. All of the gifts (talents, spiritual strengths) that individuals in the church have are designed by God for the mutual upbuilding of the community. As the old saying has it, "one hand washes the other."

But love also has to reach out beyond ourselves and the community of faith. Jesus made it clear that "Love thy neighbor" applied to everyone around us, not just to those who are neighborly toward us. He even said, "Love your enemies"!

How do we get that kind of love? We grow in *agape* love by *observing* it in Christ, *seeking to imitate* him, asking for help in *prayer*, and continuing to reckon it as ours—thus appropriating his love as a reality by an act of *faith.*

Self-Esteem. People need the healthy attitude Linus has. He says, "I think the world is so much better today than it was five years ago." Charlie Brown says, "No! How can you say that? Don't you read the papers? Don't you watch TV? The world's going to the dogs. How can you say it is a better place today than it was five years ago?" And Linus replies, "Of course the world's a better place than it was five years ago. I'm in it now!"

Do you believe that? That's one of the foundational qualities of a healthy emotional life—believing the world is a better place because you're in it. This means you've accepted yourself as a part of God's great plan for planet earth. And you cannot have a winning emotional life unless you feel that way about yourself. Only then—with that foundational sense of self-esteem—can you reach out consistently and effectively in loving relationships. (We'll look at this issue in more depth in a later chapter.)

I read recently of a fellow who said that every morning he'd get up and look in the bathroom mirror and say, "My God, do I have to depend on you for a living?"

How do *you* react to the person in your mirror? Do you believe the world is really a better place because you're here? To be a winner is to have the strength of Christ in your mind, making choices informed by the spirit of God and his Word, reaching out in *agape* love and really caring about others and yourself.

═══ THE KEY—PICK UP THE PLUMB LINE ═══

One morning, after I had given a seminar presentation on this theme, a seminar participant said to me, "Jim, when you were talking about being a successful winner, all I could think of was that you've got to be President or a millionaire, or something really big like that."

But I explained that he had misunderstood! When I talk about successful winning, I'm talking about the actual and individual "you" and about daily realistic growth. I'm not talking about some fanciful ideal or prodigious, unrealistic project.

A illustration of this is found in the Book of Zechariah. The Jews who had returned from exile in Babylon had laid the foundation for rebuilding the Temple, but they got no farther than that for fifteen years. When they finally began again, the work seemed terribly slow and progress insignificant. They were moaning, in effect, "Oh God, we've got to build that big temple, and the stones are so heavy, and there are so many of them, and it's going to take forever. . . ." And they were tempted to give up on the work their governor, Zerubbabel, had begun.

What happened? The prophet Zechariah reported a message from the Lord:

> Zerubbabel laid the foundation of this Temple, and he will complete it. (Then you will know these messages are from God, the Lord of Hosts.) *Do not despise this small beginning,* for the eyes of the Lord rejoice to see *the work begin, to see the plumbline in the hands of Zerubbabel* (4:9–10, LB, emphasis added).

To build an important edifice starts with one guy picking up a plumb line (a device used for building). And the Lord rejoices to see that one little "starting-thing" done.

William James wrote,

> I am done with great things, big things, great institutions and big success and I am for those tiny, invisible, molecular forces that work from individual to individual creeping through the crannies of the world like so many rootlets, or like the capillary oozing of water yet which if you give them time will rend the hardest monuments of man's pride.

You see, that's the way progress is usually made—with little day-by-day creeping rootlets, not huge movements.

Bonaro Overstreet wrote,

> You say the little efforts that I will make will do no good. They will never prevail to top the hovering scale where justice hangs in balance. I don't think I ever thought they would. I am prejudiced beyond debate in favor of my right to choose which side shall feel the stubborn ounces of my weight.

Here's the question to ask yourself as you begin to build a winner's mentality: "If I couldn't fail, how would I start? What one small but significant accomplishment would I begin with to start myself on a winning streak?"

Think about it with your mind, choose with your will, commit yourself to it with your emotions, and then ask, "If it were impossible to fail, what would I do first?" Then go and get with it! Do it! Now! Start! Pick up that plumb line! Press on—one small step at a time.

Papillon started it all by simply staring at the powerful, crashing waves. Then he took small, seemingly unimpressive first steps —tossing coconuts into the foam below and carefully observing what happened. He used his mind and his will and he learned, and soon his emotions were on fire as he focused on winning and escape and not on dying. He stared at waves, and then he saw Lisette, and eventually he cried out, "Man, I'm OUTAHERE!"

=== SUMMARY ===

"Success" is a lifelong process of fulfilling your potential, making and reaching important and unique goals. "Winning" is responding authentically to life by being credible, trustworthy, responsible, and genuine.

God wants you to have a winning mind—that's the way God created you from the beginning (Gen. 1). He also makes it possible for your mind to be renewed by his knowledge. We can have the mind of Christ (Phil. 2) with which we can make winning choices—informed, realistic, and authentic.

God wants you to have winning emotions. Love of God, love of neighbor, and self-esteem are the foundation stones. He wants you to get started in following his ways—use one simple ounce of energy and make the first step. Then make the second. There you go—you're on your way.

Affability: 3
The Oil of Human Relations

Affability is a specific combination of virtues that combines patience, kindness, joy, and a peaceful disposition. If you examine this constellation of attitudes, you will discover that it is very close to what Paul describes in Galatians 5:22–23 as the fruit of the Spirit: "But the fruit of the Spirit is love, joy, peace, patience, kindness, goodness, faithfulness, gentleness, self-control." A word that sums up several of these virtues is *affable*.

Affability is to human relationships what graphite is to a lock or oil to an engine. It makes relationships work better, with less friction. To be affable is to get along with people. If you care about people it is worth (and often requires) some effort to live gently and easily with them. To live affably is to get along with life! Or, as Joseph Addison wrote, "Good nature is more agreeable in conversation than wit, and gives a certain air to the countenance which is more amiable than beauty."

═══ TO BE AFFABLE IS TO BE LIKED ═══

What good looks are to the body, affability is to the personality. To be affable usually includes being liked.

Why is that necessary or valuable? Of course it isn't really necessary. It's possible to go through life and be unpopular, abrasive, and crabby. One of the paradoxes of our culture has been the way we have not only harbored and protected many eccentric grouches, but have tried somehow to plaster over their bad dispositions with a patina of quaintness to make them appear more acceptable. We have tended to excuse bad manners in some because of their genius, power, or wealth.

32

This cultural practice of ours contains a great deal of non-sense. People may indeed have other skills or talents that make them valuable, whether they are artist, engineer, or the president of the United States. But skill and talent do not really excuse an abrasive personality.

Power is another quality that is often used to excuse bad manners. A person who is powerful or celebrated seems to be able to get away with being vituperative, demanding, selfish, and/or hostile behind the scenes. Witness the behind-closed-doors exposés of the behavior of Richard Nixon, Lyndon Johnson, Henry Kissinger, and others—not to mention more recent political figures. Through memoirs and biographies such as *Mommie Dearest* (Joan Crawford), *His Way* (Frank Sinatra), and *Call Me Anna* (Patty Duke) we have learned of the abuses of power and position behind the scenes in the entertainment industry. Some who sing mellow turn into monsters when the camera fades to black!

And yet, in a way, the fact that celebrities' obnoxious personality traits *have* been hidden from public scrutiny is itself a testimonial to the value we place on affability. Take for example the cloud of silence that surrounded the boorishness of some of our recent presidents. We are disillusioned when we find public figures are small-minded or mean-spirited behind the scenes. We *want* our public figures to be nice!

Roger Ailes points this out in his fascinating book entitled *You Are the Message: Secrets of the Master Communicators.* In this book Ailes, a so-called "image expert," tells how he taught the master secrets of communication to many in business and politics—including Ronald Reagan. In fact, Ailes helped Reagan "win" a 1984 debate with Walter Mondale by showing him how to let his likability come through. Reagan, who had been declared the loser in a previous debate, learned to avert a second disaster by relaxing and being himself, by following his instincts rather than defending himself with stock answers. He even defused the issue of his age by bringing it up himself—humorously commenting that he didn't plan to make Mondale's youth and inexperience an issue in the campaign! So also in 1988, Ailes was at the center of George Bush's campaign against Michael Dukakis.

Ailes opens chapter 7 of his book by emphasizing the importance of likability to communication:

> If you could master one element of personal communications that is more powerful than anything we've discussed, it is the

quality of being *likable*. I call it the magic bullet, because if your audience likes you, they'll forgive just about everything else you do wrong. If they don't like you, you can hit every rule right on target and it doesn't matter.

Ailes acknowledges that likability is hard to define and is best understood by *avoiding* what we know people don't like—people who "complain about their problems, jabber constantly about meaningless things, and talk in a monotone. They are overly serious and rarely smile or joke about anything. They usually are self-centered." He points out that one common trait with unlikable people is arrogance or aggressiveness.*

══ AUTHENTIC AFFABILITY ══

In the face of all the stories about celebrities who are nice on the surface and bad-tempered, unprincipled, or just plain nasty behind the scenes, cynics might object that many who appear to be affable are faking—or are simply bland and without conviction. As La Rochefoucauld has observed, "Nothing is rarer than true good nature; they who are reputed to have it are generally only pliant or weak."

This is a valid concern, but no more so than with any other personality trait. Virtually any positive attitude can be faked for a time and with a segment of the population—as Lincoln pointed out about fooling people. A person can, for a time, wear a mask of joy while his or her insides are being eaten out. One who appears patient could be only manifesting weakness. But the fact that a virtue can be faked does not make it any less a virtue!

I am not recommending blandness or hypocritical smarm. What I am talking about is the great value of becoming an authentically affable person, one who is genuinely patient with people, is easily approached, is tractable, and enjoys sincere good relations with others. Authentic affability is a worthwhile goal—especially in a world where niceness is so often a façade and seeming good-nature so often a mask for weakness.

══ HOW IS AFFABILITY DEVELOPED? ══

How do you become authentically affable? One way is to develop some specific habits that will help you you cultivate qualities of affability:

*(Homewood, IL: Dow Jones Irwin, 1988), pp. 69–70.

ACCEPT PEOPLE

Practice accepting people as they are! A sure way to strain your relationships is to approach other people with an agenda for making them over—saying, in effect, "You must change in order to be recognized as a valid part of my world." (Granted, there may be some people who are so deficient that this might be a reasonable demand—but they are a lot rarer than you might think!)

The individuals who surround us are distinct and different. Each comes from a singular background and environment, and each has an individual set of habits, values, and concerns. If you can accept that fact and begin to approach people with the assumption that each has a special, valid, and worthwhile story, you can genuinely be more affable. People who are always trying to make people over with their agenda, wisdom, and experience can be a real drag.

Quite a few years ago I pastored a small mission church in Southern California—a struggling operation with just a handful of members. I was just a few years out of seminary, and this was my first calling as pastor.

Ron and Delia were a young couple who attended my church sporadically for a couple of years and then joined. They were bright professional people who were active in a number of social causes in our community. Delia was vocal and assertive—clearly the spokesperson for the family—and she had an agenda for both the church and my pastoral ministry as well. And I was just insecure enough that I bought a lot of the junk she was passing out—although I tried to be polite and friendly without necessarily accepting everything she was selling.

One day after worship, Delia took my wife and me aside and let us have it. She told us (all in Christian love, of course) all the things we were doing wrong and exactly how we were botching the job. As I look back, I realize that she was insisting on my being a kind of pastor with the kind of specific social action concerns and priorities she had for us. She wanted our church to be deeply involved with community problems which both geographically and culturally were miles away from us.

At the time, I took it all rather humbly and charitably, although inside I was really frustrated and angry. At the time I didn't fully understand why. I now understand enough about myself to know that I could never have lived up to her expectations and agenda—and I didn't want to, either. As I gradually became aware of all of this (and of the fact that I would never be able to live up to the expectations of a number of other leaders in that church) I went on to a church where I had the opportunity to minister more authentically.

The point is this: Delia wanted to be our close "friends" on a social level. We occasionally went out with them—but we never developed any kind of close friendship. I believe now that we held back because I felt I could only get along with her by my being someone other than who I was. She gave me no feeling that my perspective was accepted, valued, or respected. I did not perceive her as affable because she didn't accept me or my values.

Affability is (among other things) a function of accepting people as they are—without laying an up-front load of heavy expectations on them.

EXAMINE YOUR STEREOTYPES

Do you have a clear understanding and acceptance of your own stereotype—or, to put it another way, how you come across to people?

Many tensions develop when people perceive themselves as coming across to others one way, when they are actually coming across in a completely different way. Good friends or a small support group can be of substantial help in feeding back to you how you come across to others. The idea is to ask, "If people pigeonholed me as to 'type,' what kind of category would they put me in?" Then you can ask, "Is that how I *want* to come across?" and "What would I have to do to change that stereotype?"

To give you a start, here are a few samples of common stereotypes. Do you recognize yourself in any of them? (You can add to the list—it is intended to be suggestive, not exhaustive.)

The Successful Executive	The Macho Stud
The Parental Authority Figure	The Wet Blanket
The Bumbler	The Wallflower
Mr. Efficiency	The Sexpot
Mr. Glad-Hander	The Slob
The Rumpled Genius	Ms. Liberated Woman
The Enigmatic Greta Garbo	The Nit-Picker
Silent Sam	The Dumb Blonde
The Owl-Eyed Accountant	The Egghead, Doubledome
The Cowboy	The Rake
The Farmer	The Clod, or Klutz
The Jolly Fat Man	The Drunk

The Yuppie Junior Executive	The Frumpy Housewife
The Blue-Collar Bigot	The Jock

True, none of us likes to be stereotyped. And I'm not suggesting that stereotyping people is a good idea! But people do it as a matter of course. And the more clearly we understand how we are being typecast, the better we can adjust our demeanor to come across the way we would like to be perceived.

Almost fourteen years ago, my wife and I learned we were going to be grandparents for the first time! That was an exciting period in our lives. When we first heard the news that our daughter was pregnant, I told everyone at the office, and everyone was effusive and congratulatory. And the next day, the receptionist told me she had passed on our happy news to her husband. She said, "My husband thought it was nice that your daughter is going to have a baby. He thinks you are really the grandfatherly type."

Now, I was definitely and positively excited about our first grandchild, but I wasn't prepared to be typecast as the "grandfatherly type." After all, I was a young man of only forty-six!

Of course, Barbara insisted it was meant as a compliment—she pressed the fact that to her "the grandfatherly type" was a very good image, a very good pigeonhole in which to dwell. But to me it came as something of a cold-shower shock that anyone would see me, a mere slip of a lad just approaching the prime of life, as the "grandfatherly" type!

Still, I found it helpful to me to know just how I was seen by a segment of the population. And I might add that I have come to enjoy the label in the years that have followed.

FOCUS ON PEOPLE'S NEEDS

In John 4 we read the magnificent story of how Jesus focused on the needs of the woman at the well. In John 9 we read how he attended to the needs of the man born blind and healed him. So many people are hurting and desperately need someone who will turn toward them and care in a deliberate and redemptive way. But this takes skill—to really pay attention to the needs of others.

Focus by Listening with Care. It is one thing to hear someone speak. It is another thing to listen—to focus in and really hear what someone is trying to say.

Some years back I had the privilege of being Master of Ceremonies at a banquet at the Disneyland Hotel. The speaker for the evening was Senator Mark Hatfield of Oregon. It was one of my duties to meet the Senator at the door and escort him to his place at the dais.

That trip from front door to head table was a fascinating one. Along the way many individuals wanted to greet our distinguished guest, and he stopped to chat with more than a dozen people. Since time was short, I felt a need to keep the Senator moving along, but I soon learned that was a wasted effort on my part. As soon as Hatfield stopped to talk with an individual, his entire attention was riveted on the person at hand. It was useless to attempt to hurry him. If a person was worth stopping for, that person was worth his total focus.

I had never observed such a personally dynamic listener in my life as I saw that night. To watch Hatfield was to observe a master in the art of listening and attending with enthusiasm. When Hatfield finally did leave a person and move on to someone else, that person he had talked to knew he had received a full hearing.

Call it a political gimmick if you will, but it worked. And as I assessed it, his was a genuine interest in the needs and opinions of others. No, he didn't always agree with everyone who talked to him. But they sensed his focus was not distracted as he talked to them.

You can't come away from an encounter with that kind of person without feeling drawn to him or her. It is affirming to be really listened to by someone who counts. Senator Hatfield had learned well one of the strategic skills of affability.

Ask Questions. Another way to focus on people's needs is to ask thoughtful questions that show our interest and help us really understand the other person. It is important to learn the skills of "feeding back" to people what we are hearing, either in statement or question form. To probe gently, with appropriate questions, can show we are truly interested in understanding what the other person has to say. And this is important, because we live in a day when no one seems to really hear anyone else.

Several well-known comedians, such as Bob and Ray and Jonathan Winters, have developed routines that center around an inquiring reporter interviewing some famous celebrity. The routine never fails to break me up—even though the pattern is a familiar one. The reason it is so funny to me is that I have seen it done in real life. The reporter asks a question and is obviously not listening to the answer coming back, for as soon as the answer is completed the reporter asks a question that was just answered in the respondent's last statement.

A typical exchange goes something like this:

"Hello, I'm Sam Peterson, originally from Omaha. Now I'm living in Southern California. I've looked forward to meeting you."

"Hi there. Say, it sure is good to meet you, too. What's your name?"

"As I said, I'm Sam Peterson."

"Oh, yes. Where you from?"

"Well, I'm originally from Omaha, but about ten years ago I moved to Southern California."

"Oh, is that so? How long you been here in Southern California?"

. . . and on and on.

Good, caring questions are useful tools for focusing in on a person. Of course, if questions are misused, as above, they can be a way of conveying that we are not paying attention. Or they can be indelicate, probing, and pushy. But when they come from a genuine interest to discover the unique story that is locked in an individual's life, questions can be friendly ways of building a relationship. We like to be questioned by people who think we are interesting and worthy of acquaintance.

If you want to be an affable person, you need to learn the skills of focusing on people gently, caringly, and lovingly by asking questions to let those people know you are genuinely interested in them.

FEED IT BACK

A fourth way you can grow in affability skills is to feed back to people the good things you are hearing about them or from them. The reason that flattery (an insincere compliment) is considered a sin in the Old Testament (Psalms 12:2) is that it is the fraudulent use of a very potent tool. Genuine compliments have great and legitimate power; people like to hear good things about themselves.

Use Their Name. Most listeners like to hear their name on your lips. Every salesman is taught to catch the prospective client's name and to use it in the conversation. We like to feel people care enough to remember our name. To remember a person's name and to use it with care and love is to affirm that person's identity.

Even computer-generated letters emblazon our names in letters a half-inch high. Sometimes I actually catch myself believing, in the depths of my heart, that someone at The Publisher's Clearing House or at Reader's Digest knows me very well. At least, that's what leaps out at me from their mailings (to me and two hundred million others, I would imagine).

Feed Back the Good News. People like to hear reports of the good news you have heard about them: "Say, Mary, I hear you got promoted! That's terrific. I'm happy for you. You must be doing a good job." Even though Mary is well aware of the fact that she got promoted, it usually doesn't hurt her to know others have heard about her good news and are giving it a little air time. What are friends for, anyway? It doesn't matter how trite or old the news— if it is good news, it's a safe bet that it won't hurt to feed it back to the ones concerned.

Give Affirmation—Sincere Compliments. People like to hear sincere compliments. I emphasize the word *sincere*. It is a sin (and outright lying) to compliment people about things you don't believe in. But if you are at all sensitive you can find something to compliment almost anyone about. Such as:

> "Fred, I've always wanted to tell you how much I appreciate your smile. You have a good one—and I'm pleased to see you use it! Keep it up. It brings a ray of sunshine to the office."
>
> "Lois, that dress really looks nice on you. I've been meaning to tell you what good taste you have in your clothes."
>
> "Gail, I always feel good when you visit our corner of the office; you invariably have a twinkle in your eye. I need to tell you how much I appreciate it. Around here it really helps."
>
> "Cathy, where did you get that outstanding macramé wallhanging I saw in your living room? It sets everything off just right. What? You made it yourself? I didn't know you were into handicrafts. I bet it took a lot of work."

It may take some sensitive imagination to find something to compliment in some people. But all God's children have some worthy points that are worth commenting on. I believe all of us have a ministry of affirmation that we can fulfill if we put a little effort into it. We need good intentions—*plus some skill* and the power of God's Spirit. If we work at it—we can find something nice to say about most people.

Authentic affirmation skills and a spirit of caring are integral parts of the affability principle. People like to be around an *authentic and skilled affirmer of persons.* Like you, the reader—I think you're terrific! To have come this far in the book shows you've got great taste in picking books or great patience in plodding through uninspired prose—either one is a valuable talent. I'm impressed. (There, didn't that feel good?)

THE FRUIT OF THE SPIRIT

Affable people are those who are easily approachable and enjoyable to be with. They are not crabby, negative, and hostile. If we are filled with the Spirit of God and manifest the fruit of the Spirit— love, joy, peace, patience, kindness, goodness, faithfulness, gentleness, and self-control—we will be affable. The oil of the Spirit will lubricate our relationships with others and love will cover a multitude of sins.

══ SUMMARY ══

To be authentically affable is to be liked for the right reasons. To be affable is not to be bland or hypocritically smarmy. Affability can be developed by:

- accepting people for their uniqueness just as they are;
- understanding our own stereotype of how we come across and accepting responsibility for our typecasting or any changes we might want to make;
- focusing in on people's needs by listening with care and questioning tenderly and lovingly;
- feeding back to people an affirmation of their identity and their strengths;
- being filled with the Spirit—genuinely producing the fruit of the Spirit, which is love, joy, peace, patience, kindness, goodness, faithfulness, gentleness, self-control.

God Designed 4
You to Be Unique

> So God created . . . every living creature that moves . . . and
> every winged bird according to its kind. And God saw that it was
> good (Genesis 1:21).

God has built amazing and dramatic specialty into the animal
world. Examine the patterns of animal life, from insects to
whales, and you find incredible diversity.

Consider the homing instincts of birds that fly across oceans
to land on an island chain with pinpoint accuracy . . . the amazing timing devices built into the seventeen-year locust . . . the
sophisticated organizational structures and communication systems of bees and ants . . . the ability of many insects to communicate, through special chemicals called pheromones, up to
fifteen miles away. Incredible!

Many creatures have highly sensitive air-conditioning capabili-
ties. Bees are able to maintain an even and dependable temperature in the hive by collectively fanning their wings. And then
there's the Australian incubator bird, which uses decaying compost and cooled sand to incubate its egg. Early in the year, this
remarkable bird digs a hole ten feet deep and then gathers leaves
and other materials to fill it. The bird shapes the mouth of the
hole to gather rain for moisture, then comes back and stirs the
vegetable matter until it rots and becomes compost. The bird
uses the compost as a source of heat and uses sand, chilled at
night, for a source of cooling. The egg is placed in the hole. The
bird maintains an even 91-degree temperature for the incubating
egg by constantly restructuring the hole with warm compost or
cool sand and varying the depth of the egg in the hole.

There are ant colonies that work at such organized activities as herding aphids and capturing and colonizing slave ants. There are fish that actually fish for other fish, using a polelike appendage that grows out of their backs! And the list could go on and on.

Intricate wonder and delicacy have been built into each of the species God has created. And God's Word reveals that we also are created with a host of specialized skills, interests, talents, and gifts. We are his individual children—each one special in his sight.

=== UNIQUE ABILITIES AND VOCATIONS ===

This variety is manifested in many dimensions of life. I never cease to be amazed, for instance, at the number of ways people make a living. The educational system in which I grew up exposed us to a few traditional kinds of options: teacher, fireman, pilot, doctor, and salesman. So it has been one of the joys of my continuing education to meet people who have developed fascinating and unique ways of using their gifts to provide for their families— from collecting used grease from restaurants to brokering railroad cars full of potatoes to designing high-tech "clean rooms" for the computer industry.

Whenever I discover people who have interesting vocations, I love to take them aside and "pick their brains" to find out how they got started in their line of work. In my former church, there were quite a few men who were owners of their own companies. I realized that because our church was very large (three-thousand-plus members), many of these fellows did not know the others. So I got them all together for lunch, just so they could get to know each other. I invited ten men, and I explained my idea that they would have a great deal in common by virtue of the fact that each headed up his own company. Then I asked each to tell the story of how he had originally entered into and then built up his business.

Each man told his story. Ralph owned the local rubbish collection company. Steve owned three McDonald's® hamburger restaurants. Bob built seismic instruments, including some that are still on the moon. Jim ran a direct mail business. Ron fabricated piston rods for race cars. Russ owned an advertising agency and television production company. Jack owned a steel fabricating company. Clair owned a Ford agency. Bill marketed pool-cleaning supplies across several states.

It was one of the most fascinating two hours I have ever spent. Each man had arrived at his present vocational situation by means of a distinct set of experiences. Some had come the academic route, with B.A.s and M.B.A.s. A few hadn't gone much past high school. Some had gone through five or six different vocational changes before finding their niche.

Some of the men I invited to that lunch were quiet, some extroverts. On the surface they had little in common. But all liked to work and liked what they were doing. And they also shared an exciting and positive outlook on life. Even though they had come from different backgrounds, they all were extremely interested in other people, new ways of doing things, different perspectives. None of them was provincial or narrow-minded. They were individualists whose minds were open to others, who were willing to listen and to learn from others. Each was unique—just as you and I are each unique.

BIBLICAL EXAMPLES OF HUMAN UNIQUENESS

The Bible abounds with descriptions of the different gifts and abilities God provides his children. Exodus 35 and 36, for example, contain the fascinating account of the appointment of workmen to build the tabernacle in the wilderness. We read of Bezalel, whom God had filled with his Spirit and "with ability, with intelligence, with knowledge, and with all craftsmanship, to devise artistic designs, to work in gold and silver and bronze, in cutting stones for setting, and in carving wood, for work in every skilled craft" (35:30–33). Bezalel was given help in the person of Oholiab and other men who could do the work of a "workman or skilled designer" (v. 35). And all the children of Israel donated their special talents, such as spinning fine thread (v. 25–26) toward constructing the tabernacle.

And there are dozens of other instances in the Bible of the many different ways a person's unique abilities can be used in vocational service. Elsewhere in Exodus, for example, we read that the task of judging the people and settling their disputes became too much for Moses, who was handling the job alone. So his father-in-law, Jethro, advised Moses to find and appoint men to share the work. Jethro said, "Choose able men from all the people, such as fear God, men who are trustworthy and who hate a bribe; and place such men over the people as rulers of thousands, of hundreds, of fifties, and of tens. And let them judge the people at all times. . . . Moses chose able men out of all Israel" (Exod. 18:21, 25).

The list could go on and on. In the Book of Daniel, we read of the four Hebrew youths to whom "God gave . . . learning and skill in all letters and wisdom; and Daniel had understanding in all visions and dreams" (Dan. 1:17). As a result of his special gifts, Daniel was appointed a counselor to the Babylonian king.

So also the Bible tells of women with unique gifts and abilities. There was Deborah, who was one of the judges over Israel. There was the "virtuous woman" described in Proverbs 31, who bought real estate and marketed handmade garments as well as looking after her household. There was Martha, who excelled as a cook and a hostess, and her sister, Mary, who had the spiritual sensitivity to sit for hours and listen at Jesus' feet. And of course there was Mary, Jesus' mother, who found fulfillment in her role of wife and mother—and Priscilla, who worked along with her husband as a tentmaker and was a pillar of the early church. Each story is singular; and each person had a unique niche to fill.

APPRECIATING YOUR UNIQUE POSSIBILITIES

In my counseling over the years, I have been amazed at the number of people who do not appear to appreciate the wide variety of people there are and the wide spectrum of opportunities life offers. I often counsel with people who are depressed and upset because they feel that they have been painted into a corner by their circumstances. They see few options for themselves either for vocation or for doing things differently in their marriage or in their family.

If there is any topic that needs to be stressed more in schools and also within the church, it is the topic of vocational and personal variety and uniqueness. We need to open up people's horizons, broaden their vision, help them to see that there are many unique possibilities in life—whether it is raising kids, earning a living, organizing their families, or what-have-you. We are each unique. And each of us has a particular niche—or several niches —where we can display and use the unique set of talents and abilities God has given us.

═══ YOUR UNIQUE RHYTHM ═══

Just as each of us has a unique set of gifts and abilities, we each have our own built-in "clock"—a kind of rhythm that determines what hours are most productive for us. Although our modern industrial society tries to mold us all into an "eight to five" carbon-copy lifestyle and also suggests that's how all "right thinking" persons should live, "eight to five" is not the only productive time schedule!

While I was in college and seminary I worked a variety of schedules, including both swing (4:30 P.M. to 1:00 A.M.) and graveyard shifts (9:00 P.M. to 6:00 A.M.). Those experiences taught me that life can be lived in other than the typical eight-to-five framework.

I have always been fascinated by the various time schedules some people work on. Lorin Hollander is a concert pianist who does about ninety-five concerts a year. He practices from four to six hours a day, and his practice period may start as early as three in the morning. That schedule fits his unique lifestyle. It works for him.

My late dear friend Ken Johnson was a freelance copywriter. He tended to work in bursts. When he was "hot" and writing prolifically, he would frequently work from about nine in the evening until five or six in the morning for three to five days in a row. Then at other times he would write during the daylight hours. Ken would have gone crazy if he had to sit in an office cubicle and write from eight in the morning until five at night! He had an individual—if erratic—style and schedule that worked for him.

(I would add parenthetically another story about my friend Ken's uniqueness. After his wife died and he had to take over the management of the checkbook, he discovered that monthly balancing took far more time than he was willing to give—and never gave satisfactory results. So he set up two checking accounts. He would use one until it was fully messed up, and then he would shift to the other for two or three months until all the checks had cleared in the first one. Then he would accept the bank's total on the first account and go back to it while the second account—now in chaos—fell into place. This way he avoided ever having to reconcile either checking account fully. Ken was a true original!)

In my first twenty years of ministry, I was by inclination and choice a "night person" who was not at my best early in the morning. The "off-hour" jobs I took during college and seminary introduced me to life at night, and that schedule stuck for a long time. Since the model for ministers, promulgated in seminary, was that of the married monk—up before dawn for four hours of prayer before the city awakes—I had a hard time getting into that schedule, and I was fascinated by other "night people" who succeeded in articulating their preference. One of my favorites is playwright and director Moss Hart, who makes the case for night people in a passage from his autobiography, *Act One:*

> There is ample evidence, I am certain, that the early morning hours are the golden ones for work, and the testimony of such loiterers as myself on the enduring joys of late-rising carries little weight with folk who are up and about at dawn, busily improving those shining early hours. They continue to have my blessing from the depths of a warm and skeptical bed. I accept their data on the beauties of the early morning along with their thinly veiled scorn of my own pitiable indolence; but the truth is, I have never been able to understand the full extent of my loss.
>
> The Bay of Naples and the harbor at Rio de Janeiro were still there at one o'clock in the afternoon when I first laid eyes on them, and were even more beautiful, it seemed to me, for my being wide awake and thoroughly refreshed when I did look upon them. So far as I know, anything worth hearing is not usually uttered at seven o'clock in the morning; and if it is, it will generally be repeated at a more reasonable hour for a larger and more wakeful audience. Much more likely, if it is worth hearing at all, it will be set down in print where it can be decently enjoyed by dawdling souls, like myself, who lumpishly resist the golden glow of dawn.*

Articulate as Moss Hart's argument is, I am not saying you should follow it—any more than I would insist you need to "rise and shine" every morning at five in the morning. My point is that you need to find your own rhythm—the best time schedule for you, in your context of life—and not be intimidated by those who would suggest your way of doing things is less valid than theirs.

The great pressure against living out one's own authentic time schedule comes from the strictures of the bureaucracies most of us work in—which tend to force people into common molds. This is true even in the church, where people tend to build expectations for one another that may or may not be helpful or realistic.

I believe we need more and more to become that kind of authentic persons who can press for and reach realistic compromises with the demands of those around us. I confess I have always admired people who take the risk and refuse to be intimidated—to be painted in a corner by the fact that most of the world (including most jobs) operate on an eight-to-five schedule. It may take a little

*Moss Hart, *Act One* (New York: Random House, 1958), pp. 299–300.

doing, but there are ways to build a productive life around your own unique rhythm.

ADJUSTING YOUR RHYTHM

Now all this is not to say that your unique time schedule cannot be adjusted! Even though it's important to appreciate your body's "clock" and not be intimidated by the world around you, it is also important to realize that it *is* possible to change your rhythm if your goals and values demand it.

Interestingly enough, inspired as I was by Moss Hart's vision of sunrise, about ten years ago I changed into a morning person through a series of circumstances! Now I find my most productive time for study and writing long before noon.

It's all a matter of thinking out what is important to you. Every particular lifestyle has its price, and that cost must be counted. If you want to be a police officer, you have to come to terms with the unique schedule of that profession—if you want a nice orderly five-day-a-week, forty-hour schedule, don't be a cop! And the same is true of making the choice to become a doctor, lawyer, mother, pastor, or proprietor of your own bike rental outlet at the beach!

The key is understanding that whatever vocational or lifestyle choice you make, you must take the responsibility for accepting the "givens" of that choice. The feeling of helplessness so many people experience grows out of the feeling that they have been coerced by circumstances beyond their control. A sense of control begins with understanding what your authentic life should be and then making choices and the preparation that will bring you to that desired place.

═══ TAKING RESPONSIBILITY ═══

If there is any message that I am trying to get across, it is simply this: It is your responsibility to come to terms with your unique abilities and opportunities, to count the cost, and then to make the changes that will improve your life. You can make no change in your life and your lifestyle without first accepting the responsibility for making the change. And those choices must be made with a realistic appraisal of the factors involved.

There are all sorts of excuses, of course, for failing to make the choices that will improve our lives. One of the most common is "But I'm too old!" That is one of the tiredest, most overworked cop-outs around. And it is given the lie by the fact that, down through history, men and women have radically changed their lives again and again, even after reaching maturity.

Joseph Conrad didn't even learn to speak English until he was in his forties, and then he went on to become a classic English novelist. George Burns began a whole new career as a single performer after the death of his wife, Gracie Allen, when he was sixty-eight years old. And as I write this, he is in his nineties and still going strong!

On every hand we see people's lives changing radically— marriage, graduation, death, divorce, the birth of a child, aging, loss of income, promotions, having to move to another part of the country. In all of this, we can see ourselves as inert victims or we can take the opportunity to discover unique new patterns for our lives—particularly new rhythms and time schedules.

Lee and Lane Barker, a young couple in our church, have been married six and a half years. He is a high-tech photographer here in the Silicon Valley; she is a marriage counselor. Both of their sets of parents live in another state. Up until last summer, they had been childless; then they had triplets! Our church has helped them for several months now by sending over two people every day from about eleven in the morning until about two or three in the afternoon (five days a week) to care for little Max, Mollie, and Lindsay. During that time slot, Lane either takes a nap or runs errands. She has developed a whole new time schedule during this period that fits these circumstances. The Barkers plan to move closer to their parents back home when arrangements can be made. They will continue to modify their patterns of life as the triplets grow older and when they are closer to their families again.

It has been a joy to see these two young people take command of their lives with this new reality. I remember talking to them the day after they learned Lane was going to have triplets. Naturally, they were overwhelmed, and there were tears. Now, they have had T-shirts printed up that read, "Yes, We're Glad They're Not Yours, Too!"

To have an affable, confident relationship with life means to come to grips with what works for you—now—today! God has given you the choice of what you do with your life. Be aware that there are indeed many options, many alternatives, many possibilities besides being a fireman, a pilot, a teacher, or an "eight to five" office worker.

COMING TO TERMS WITH
YOUR UNIQUE STAGE OF LIFE

One of the strategic truths that a person needs to get hold of in order to live a successful and confident life is that change is inevitable. Therefore, change should be not only accepted, but also welcomed as a part of God's design.

Our lives do keep changing, whether we accept that change or not. I was reminded of this when talking to a friend about changing my will. I have had to do this several times in my adult life because my circumstances keep changing. At one point in my life, for example, I had four children at home, ranging from toddlers to teenagers. Today all my children are adults—and each one of them is in a different situation. The needs of a sixth grader are very different from those of an adult, and my will needs to change accordingly. My friend pointed out that the average person has to rewrite his will on the average of about every seven years—some must do it more often.

As children are born, grow, and become self-sufficient; as grandchildren and great-grandchildren arrive; as deaths occur within the family, things change. Rather than fighting the changes in each stage of life, we should welcome them as part of reality.

CELEBRATE TODAY!

I remember so clearly the summer our daughter, Beverly, spent a vacation weekend with us and brought along our first grandchild, John. He was just two months old, and we all had a wonderful time admiring him. Now John is almost thirteen, and his nine-year-old brother, Tim, is tagging along behind. And we still have a wonderful time.

Each stage of life is unique and wonderful! So many parents are too busy wishing their little one would hurry up and be a year old . . . or learn to walk . . . or start to school . . . or be able to drive. Those changes will come and they should be welcomed. But along the way, each stage of life should be celebrated.

Celebrate *today* even in its transitory moment. Last night we were invited to dinner along with our associate pastor and his wife and their little three-month-old baby girl, Hayden. We spent a good deal of time after dinner admiring the marvel of that tiny infant, so full of potential and wonder. I urged them to cherish these moments of her infancy—for she will continue to change, and this special time will soon pass. The point is this—no one stage of life should be preferred over another. Each stage has its own unique glories to be enjoyed.

I can remember thinking when I was in high school that this was just about the most exciting and best of all possible worlds. Hormones were coursing through my body, causing feelings I had never experienced before; girls were becoming a marvel before my eyes. My friends were clever and wise. I almost lamented leaving that kaleidoscopic cocoon of puberty. But now that I have lived through a few other stages, I realize that, nifty as I perceived those years to be, I wouldn't want to relive them for anything! There were other and better things ahead.

I recently attended the fortieth reunion of my class at West Seattle High School in the state of Washington. What a Twilight-Zone experience that was! I had never been back to any reunion during all those years. It was amazing to see people I had not seen since the day we graduated, people I had gone to school with from kindergarten all the way through twelfth grade. Talk about cosmic changes!

But God created us to live through changes. Each one of the stages we go through is unique. Discover them. Use them. Exploit them. Develop them.

COMING TO TERMS WITH AGING

As I have approached the close of my fifties, I have been particularly sensitive to the process of aging. I have spent time with older people in various situations. I am impressed that by and large we are responsible for the kind of elderly people we become. I suspect it is no surprise that some of us end up crabby and alone. We make decisions in life that prepare us either well or poorly for old age.

Some time back, I had the opportunity of calling regularly on two women in very similar situations. Both were eighty-three years old, and they had broken their hips within a week or so of each other. Both had only sons who lived out of the area and therefore were not close by during their convalescence. And both were widows who normally lived alone and were modestly well-off. Yet the responses of these two women to these similar sets of circumstances were as different as night and day.

The one lady, Meta, could not praise the doctors and nurses enough. She saw them as God's ministers caring for her in her difficult time. Her attitude on my every visit was one of radiant gratitude that she could be in such a nice hospital with such good care. She always thanked me profusely for coming to visit, recognizing I had a busy schedule, and told me how thoughtful it was of me to take time for her. Her attitude was radiant; she was looking forward to getting well and getting back to normal.

Meta was accepting of life and the stage of life she was in. Her son was out of the area because he had a strategic job offer to take his family to Europe to teach. He had tried to cancel his appointment to be with his mother, but she would hear none of it; she had sent him and his family off with sincere blessings. As I would come into her room she would smile from ear to ear and reach for the latest postcard or letter from her grandson or granddaughter. She was thrilled with their experiences in Europe and rejoicing in their good fortune. In fact, the very focus of her attitude on her children's good fortune took her mind off her present infirmities.

The other lady—we'll call her Vivian—was a different story altogether. She was dependent, whiny, and clinging, full of self-pity. Those who visited her felt she was trying to load all her problems and the responsibility for solving them on their shoulders. Her attitude was that of a petulant child looking for someone to take over her life and work things out for her. Of course, there were those who were trying to help her out. But nothing ever seemed to satisfy her. To hear her talk, hers was the most desperate situation anyone had ever been in; hers was a case worthy of congressional action. She would have had you spooning the food into her mouth if you would.

In talking to people like Vivian, one can get the idea that aging must necessarily be a tragic process for all. These people, perhaps because they have done a poor job of preparing emotionally for old age, assume that, after a certain point, decline and decay are all but inevitable and universal.

I have never really accepted that, even though I am keenly aware that there are often debilitating circumstances and illnesses that affect the aged. (As Art Linkletter has written, "Growing old is not for sissies.") Perhaps this is because throughout my life I have known older people who were vital, involved participants in the life around them.

When I was a boy of five or six, Margaret Munns was the oldest person I knew, but she had a great outlook on life. For many years she had been an international officer of the Women's Christian Temperance Union, and she would visit us about once or twice a year while she was still active in her office—well up into her seventies. She had traveled widely throughout the world during her lifetime. She was positive and assertive, able to discuss cogently any world issue that came up. The one thing that I carried away from her was that it was no tragedy to be elderly. She always impressed me with her sensitivity, her selflessness, her alertness, her generosity, and her ability to enjoy life.

Louise Carlson, my mother-in-law, was that kind of person, too. We lived with my in-laws while I was in seminary and while I served at my first church. Later, after my father-in-law died, Louise lived with us for fourteen years until she passed away at age eighty-three. She and I did not always see eye to eye on issues political, theological, or cultural. But she was a bright, generous, loving mother-in-law and an outstanding grandmother to our children. She saw it as her task to contribute to our family life so that my wife and I were able to engage in many church activities we would not otherwise have been able to enjoy. She washed and ironed clothes, she cooked, she did dishes, she mended socks, she proofread my papers, she corrected our grammar, she loved to talk about the meaning of lesser-used words. She made a valuable place for herself in our family. She gave constantly of herself —and with sincerity.

Louise constantly demonstrated that to be old is not to be an inactive spectator of life. She lived a contributive life. With the exception of the two months of illness prior to her death, she was a bright-eyed participant in our family life. Yes, she had some of the normal physical limitations and breakdowns when her health failed. She had some limitations that changed with the years. But she never used those as an excuse to become self-indulgent or passive. She used her old age as a period of contribution.

MAKING THE MOST OF
WHAT LIFE GIVES YOU

What stage are you in your life? Single adult? Young married? Middle-age? Senior citizen? That's a stage to explore and exploit. Do not view it as a tragedy, but as an opportunity to grow in some new way, to meet some friends you would never have met otherwise.

And the same is true of any of the unique circumstances of your life—whether it be a talent or a handicap, a unique family background, a geographical location, or any other set of circumstances.

This point was impressed upon me one night in 1976. I had been watching a good deal of the 1976 Democratic Convention in

New York on television, and I was particularly looking forward to the keynote address of Senator John Glenn of Ohio, the former astronaut.

The other co-keynoter was Representative Barbara Jordan of Texas, and frankly, I felt sorry for her. How would you like to follow the act of an astronaut, a hero, a senator? He had it all going for him. And who had heard of Barbara Jordan?

As it turned out, Glenn delivered what he termed a "substantive" speech rather than one full of razzle-dazzle. I had to keep splashing my face with cold water to keep awake. And then the Black lady from Texas came on. I hadn't planned to listen to her speech, so I turned the TV off.

Later that night, I heard a recap of the program, and I began to hear about her great speech and the amazing response she had received. And I had the opportunity of hearing a good portion of her speech on the reruns. Wow! She had charisma. She knocked the ball out of the park. She was not intimidated by the fact that she was following a genuine hero—an astronaut, Mr. Clean, Jack Armstrong, the All-American boy. She did her thing and she did it well, and she made his speech look weak by contrast. The commentators referred to Glenn's speech as "lackluster," and the gossip was that whereas Glenn was one of the top contenders for the Vice President spot, now Glenn had slipped to no higher than third choice.

So often we find ourselves in a spot like that of Barbara Jordan —a situation where we will be following a really tough act or facing a really tough challenge. But we can learn from her. She didn't try to top anybody; she just did a fabulous job of being herself—an articulate Black lady politician from Texas who had something to say. She accepted the moment and the situation that was there and made something out of it.

This is the way we need to view our changing lives. We need to bloom where we are planted. We need to take the spot we have been given or the stage where we are in life, and we need to polish it up—let it shine today. And tomorrow we need to be prepared for something new and different.

══ SUMMARY ══

God made you unique. As *Saturday Night Live*'s "Church Lady" would ask, "Aren't you something special?" And the answer is an unequivocal "YES!" In the billions of years of time that the astronomers say they can compute—there has only been *one* of you. Cherish the incredible opportunity of your singular life. As you discover the great value of your particular identity and mission, you will be able to relate to people with a much more affable and confident demeanor.

Friend, it is the unique YOU that is standing there at the edge of the cliff along with Papillon, facing your unique opportunities. Go ahead—leap into the surf, catch Lisette, and ride to freedom!

God Wants You 5
to Experience Abundance

God wants you to experience abundance in your life. *In a sense,* God wants you to be rich. Jesus said, "I am come that they may have life, and have it *abundantly*" (John 10:10). To be rich or have abundance is to have in excess, more than is needed—or, as Jesus said, "Pressed down, shaken together, running over" (Luke 6:38).

God's Word teaches that each of us is to be rich in his or her own special way. We each have gifts and opportunities that no one else has. The sooner we find out precisely where our prospects for unique richness are located, the more confident and affable our lives can be.

What does it mean to lead a rich life? Strangely enough, in a very important way, it means to be content with the riches we already have! William Ellery Channing, a nineteenth-century clergyman, wrote,

> To live content with small means, to seek elegance rather than luxury and refinement rather than fashion; to be worthy not respectable. . . . to study hard, think quietly, talk gently, act frankly; to listen to the stars and birds, to babes and sages with open heart; to bear all cheerfully, do all bravely, await occasions, hurry never; in a word, to let the spiritual, unbidden and unconscious grow up through the common.

The ancient rabbis put it this way: "Who is rich? Only the man who rejoices in his portion, that is, the contented man."

Perhaps no better explanation has been found than the one discovered by Grandpa Tubbs in a story told by Dr. Louis Binstock. Grandpa Tubbs had been stubborn and crabbed for years. No one in the village could please him. Then, overnight, he changed. Now only sweetness and light radiated from his personality.

The villagers were astounded. "Grandpa," they asked, "what is it that caused you to change so suddenly?"

"Well," the old man replied, "I've been striving all my life for a contented mind. It's done no good. So I've just decided to be contented without it."

Indeed, there are many ways to define the experience of abundance. I would suggest three characteristics of such a life.

═══ *RICH IN VARIETY* ═══

William Cowper wrote, "Variety is the very spice of life, that gives it all its flavor." I can't imagine anyone wanting to live a dull life or one that is full of boring sameness. We all need a change of pace from time to time.

Unfortunately, many people think that we can only achieve variety in our lives through expensive means. Not so. One does not need to visit the Swiss Alps or Bora Bora to get an enhancing change of pace. There are many easily affordable and close-at-hand methods of achieving the richness of diversity. Let me suggest a few practical ones:

Take a Walk. Take an evening stroll in a completely different part of town. Take a "cheap, cheap" walking tour as a means of getting to know your community. You will see things by going on foot that you would never see otherwise.

Stop along the way and meet people. You may be surprised at the new friends you meet. My brother, Warren, was a cadet at King's Point Merchant Marine Academy during World War II. The cadets occasionally went on walking tours among the lovely Long Island mansions near the Point. One day, on one of their jaunts, he and some of his friends were invited into the home of one of the richest oil families in the nation. They met people they would otherwise never have known.

Now, your walking tours probably won't take you into the parlors of the wealthy; more likely they will lead you past the local 7-11 store or the pool hall. But take a friend with you and take a stroll where you have never been. Make friends with your environs. Enjoy the variety and abundance that surrounds you!

If you want to really get inspired about the rich possibilities of walking, read Peter Jenkins's fascinating books about his walking tours—first across America and later across other parts of the world—even China! You may not want to walk *that* far, but you will come to appreciate the experiences a walking tour can bring.*

Issue a Spontaneous Invitation. Spontaneously invite some people over on a warm evening for homemade ice cream. I've found that if you tell people you are making homemade strawberry ice cream, you will rarely get turned down. So often people don't get around to entertaining because a dinner party is such a big undertaking. Many people don't want to entertain unless they can put out the best china and serve a standing prime rib roast. And because that's so much trouble and costs so much, they don't get around to doing it very often. So, do a bit of last-minute, "come on home with us after church and share some ice cream" type of entertaining. By making it spontaneous, you don't have to worry for three days about getting the house cleaned before the company comes.

Put Together a Caravan. A couple of times we have been sitting around the house on a warm summer evening and suddenly decided to jump in our car, collect two or three couples without any prior warning, and make a caravan down to the local pie shop (in our area, Marie Callendar's). Just keep knocking on your friends' doors until you get a pie shop quorum. And, of course, you could also go for frozen yogurt or chocolate cookies. It is best to limit this to those whose children are old enough to be left alone for an hour—or, what the heck, invite the kids along.

Do Something for the First Time. Plan to do something this month that you have never done before. Usually the Calendar section of the Sunday Paper will list everything that is going on in your community—the local college presentation of *As You Like It*, the lapidary show, the dog show, the auto convention, an art festival, a sand-castle building contest . . . and on and on. Investigate the culture of your community and do something beyond the ordinary. Surprise yourself.

One night a colleague of mine asked us to go out to a local young-adult-oriented night club in Pasadena. I had never been to such a place before. It cost us very little to get in—and we had a

*Peter Jenkins, *A Walk across America* (New York: Fawcett Crest, 1979); Peter and Barbara Jenkins, *The Walk West: A Walk across America 2* (New York: Fawcett Crest, 1981); Peter and Barbara Jenkins, *The Road Unseen* (Nashville: Thomas Nelson, 1985); Peter Jenkins, *Across China* (New York: Fawcett Crest, 1986).

marvelous time of fellowship and fairly decent pizza, to boot. And, in addition, we heard some great close-harmony quartet singing.

Do Something Nice. Do something out of the blue for a friend. So much of the time, our friendly gestures are deeply channeled into ruts. We find ourselves doing things for those we care about because it is their birthday, Mother's Day, Graduation Day, or some other obvious occasion. But just doing something nice for someone is a way of saying to them, "Hey, you are terrific, and I want you to know I think you are something else—so here's a cake (or a new scarf, or a screwdriver, or a six pack of Diet Cola) *just for you.*" Maybe you surprise a shut-in friend by mowing the lawn for him or her. Or you could take an elderly relative for a ride. Or send a funny card. The possibilities are endless.

Make a Friend. If you are like many people, you have just drifted into your friendships over a period of time. And that's OK—as one method. But do you ever put your sights on some new people and say, "This week I am going to try to get to know those people a little better"? The making of new friends as a normal part of your lifestyle brings variety into your life. "A man that hath friends must shew himself friendly" (Prov. 18:24, KJV).

Learn a Skill. Learn to hook a rug, or read Sanskrit, or bowl over 100, or catch a fish, or play chess. There are thousands of skills, interests, and hobbies that can bring variety to one's life.

People who are proficient in a skill are usually willing to share their expertise with a novice. This is also a good way to make friends. Say to a person, "Hey, I would like to learn about tying flies (or tossing pottery, or programming a computer, or what have you), and I understand you are really good at this. Could you give me an evening or two to start me off on the right foot?"

Part of the excitement of God's creation is to be found in the fact that there is such a great variety of interests and skills available for us to focus on. And in the doing of these we meet all kinds of people and find opportunity to expand our lives to greater and greater potential.

Plan a Trip. Notice I did not just say, "Take a trip"! You get a good deal more "variety mileage" out of a trip by planning it well in advance and enjoying the tasty fruits of anticipation with another friend.

Say you are going on a motor trip to the Gold Rush country in California. Go to the library and learn about the history of the area. Get out a map; locate Sutter's Mill and Sonora and Angel's

Camp. Learn about Black Bart and Mark Twain and the role of the Chinese in those Gold Rush days. Brush up on your history of antiques, because the Mother Lode country is filled with antique stores. Better yet, invite someone over who's been there before and "pick his brain."

A few years ago, my wife, Avis, and I had the privilege of leading our first trip to the Holy Land. And we found that one of the most enriching parts of the trip came in the planning and mutual anticipation of these trips. Our program offered courses in the geography, topography, and history of the cities where we were to travel, and those courses enriched our travel experience immensely.

Whether you are thinking about a short drive to a nearby town or a two-month junket around the country with a trailer or a flight halfway around the world, you can add variety and enrichment to your experience by laying the trip out well in advance and planning it with others.

Do Something You Haven't Had Time For. Reach back into that dusty old bag of things that you have been planning to get done. Take one thing out, dust it off, put a little shine on it, and set it before you as a goal to be accomplished in the next week, or month, or year (whichever is most appropriate). This could include such things as visiting a nearby tourist attraction, cleaning out the garage or attic, writing six sonnets, visiting your three old-maid aunts, or studying for a real estate license. Then make a little chart with a checklist of the steps on a day-by-day or weekly basis to get it done. Watch the chart fill up as you check off the steps.

Hang a Light in Your Tunnel. Life can be lived more abundantly by introducing some variety into it. We all need a change of pace to lighten the load and bring some freshness into our vision. If there's no light at the end of your tunnel, take the responsibility to hang one up yourself.

Each year Avis and I plan at least one short winter outing to visit the snow and a trip to the desert in the spring or the fall. (This is possible if you live in California.) These mini-breaks are planned so we always have something to look forward to. It's amazing how hard you can work if you know there's something good coming up just around the corner.

RICH IN HEALTH

Besides variety, richness can also come from an awareness of your unique state of strength and health. I say unique because as a matter of fact one's health or body strength is a very special and precious commodity. So often we hear people describing their level of health only in terms of what they *can't* do.

The out-of-shape may lament that they can't walk or run as fast or as far, or lift as much, or bend as easily as someone else—or as easily as they once could. But whatever your level of health, if you are healthy enough to read this book (or even hear it read to you), you have your own unique level of strength and health that equips you to do *something*. To discover and fulfill that set of unique things that you can do, and to do that with a sense of gratitude and praise to God, is to discover *richness* in your life.

Perhaps your level of health won't permit you to run the hundred-yard dash in ten seconds. So what, if it allows you to iron a shirt, or draw a plan, or map a county, or cane a chair, or knit a sweater? Those are certainly just as valid ways of functioning—and probably much more appreciated—than running frantic dashes in your skivvies all around town, scaring the horses and endangering traffic!

Rather than sitting around depressed because we aren't all built like Arnold Schwarzenegger, or as disciplined as Jack La Lanne, or as well preserved as Elizabeth Taylor, we need to explore and develop those areas of health that *are* available to us as unique individuals. Here are a few practical suggestions in this area of health:

Walking. Until recently, walking was probably the most neglected form of exercise in the world. Now, in the wake of injuries from more strenuous sports, it seems to be enjoying a resurgence of popularity. No, walking probably won't prepare you for the Boston marathon, but it will enhance your life. By itself it won't necessarily make you lose weight (if it were, my mailman would be slender instead of portly), but it can improve your fitness level with a minimal chance of injury.

Prayer and Meditation on God's Word. Simply putting aside the trash and the clamor of the day, letting your mind relax, and opening yourself to the slow-paced consideration of a selected portion of Scripture, will clear your mind and lower your stress level. This in turn can have a remarkably beneficial effect on your physical as well as spiritual health—our bodies need deep relaxation as much as our spirits need God's Word.

Deep Breathing. Very few of us use our lungs to full capacity. Much information on this subject has been developed in recent days in conjunction with a variety of relaxation techniques. Check with your local library for books on how to do such exercises.

Eating Right. Good nutrition is something many of us are aware of these days—but statistics show that many of us are not acting on that awareness. Start working on the quality of your food. Cut down on fats, excessive protein (meats), and simple sugars, and bolster your menu with more fresh fruit and vegetables, complex carbohydrates, and fiber. For an outstanding understanding of the really healthy diet, pick up a copy of *The McDougall Plan,** or get a copy of the Pritikin diet.

Regular Medical Care. Proper health care, including occasional complete check-ups, is a sign of taking responsibility for our bodies. Common medical sense tells us that many ailments can be nipped in the bud if they are caught early.

Building an Atmosphere of Caring and Affection. The general "tone" of our home and work environment makes an important difference in our health. To live in an atmosphere of criticism, tension, stress, and rancor is to ask for ulcers, high blood pressure and heart attack. If you find yourself stuck in that kind of environment, you need to make some changes. You cannot expect to maintain good health in the midst of constant tension, anymore than you would expect to smell like a rose after working in a sewer. If, over the long haul, you live in such an atmosphere, you have made a choice to live your life going uphill all the way. Sometimes the best and wisest change is simply to move to a different environment. Even though such a move may be costly, the alternative in terms of health can be even more costly.

The abundant life is one that is rich in health, particularly in healthy attitudes. This is not necessarily health as someone else finds it, or as you had it ten years ago, but health as uniquely available to you now by God, in which your special strengths are being used and developed.

=== RICH IN MATERIAL WEALTH? ===

What about abundance in terms of money and material possessions? Is it good or bad to be financially rich?

We have all heard arguments on both sides. There are those who defend the idea that God wants Christians to go "first class" and that material wealth is an almost inevitable outgrowth of faith. (Certainly the excesses of recent notorious television

*(Piscataway, NJ: New Century Publishers, 1983).

evangelists have brought disrepute to much of this "God wants you to be a millionaire by sending me your money" thinking.)

On the other hand, there are those who quote Jesus' saying that it is easier for a camel to get through the eye of a needle than for a rich man to get into heaven. Therefore, they say, it must follow that we should be suspicious of ever having any substantial amount of money or material goods. According to this thinking, one must obviously be poor to be righteous.

Certainly there are several biblical passages that suggest that the dollar (and all of the things that go with it) can wreak havoc in our lives. Paul says, for instance, that "those who desire to be rich fall into temptation, into a snare, into many senseless and hurtful desires that plunge men into ruin and destruction," and he goes on to say that "the love of money is the root of all evil" (1 Tim. 6:9–10).

Beyond question, such passages teach clearly that the greedy pursuit of wealth as an end in itself is a dead-end street that will betray us in the long run (and in some cases even in the short run). But that is not the total teaching of the Bible on wealth.

For although the Bible soundly condemns the selfish pursuit of riches, it also recognizes the many practical benefits financial resources make possible. And it does not deny that wealth and good fortune are in many cases a reward to be enjoyed. That riches are not everything does not mean they are nothing. That riches *can* be a trap does not mean they are always a trap.

A full study of the Bible's teaching on material wealth reveals many dimensions. In the Old Testament, the promise of material enrichment was used as a carrot in front of the children of Israel as they were about to go into the Promised Land. Moses, speaking for God, declared the blessings that would follow obedience if the people of God truly followed him—and those blessings were not described in other-worldly, wholly spiritual terms. Rather, the promised blessings of obedience included such down-to-earth items as ample crops, large flocks and herds, fruit, and bread: "The Lord will bless you with good crops and healthy cattle, and prosper everything you do when you arrive in the land the Lord your God is giving you" (Deut. 28:8, LB).

The wisdom literature of the Old Testament shows that the covenant people had great respect for financial prosperity. The building up of wealth was seen as legitimate when it was the result of diligence and hard work. The opposite traits, such as sloth, often brought poverty:

Go to the ant, O sluggard;
  consider her ways, and be wise.
Without having any chief,
  officer or ruler,
she prepares her food in summer,
  and gathers her sustenance in harvest.
How long will you lie there, O sluggard?
  When will you arise from your sleep?
A little sleep, a little slumber,
  a little folding of the hands to rest,
and poverty will come upon you like a vagabond,
  and want like an armed man (Prov. 6:6–11).

The Hebrews of Old Testament times also saw the accumulation of wealth to be the *result* of *wise choices* in life (such as mingling with the right kinds of righteous people), while poverty was the result of laziness and sin:

He who walks with wise men becomes wise,
  but the companion of fools will suffer harm.
Misfortune pursues sinners,
  but *prosperity rewards the righteous*. . . .
The righteous has enough to satisfy his appetite,
  but the belly of the wicked suffers want (Prov. 13:21–23, 25,
    emphasis mine).

By the same token, the Old Testament recognized that there were those who got their wealth by treachery and stealth, and there was bad news for them:

The getting of treasures by a lying tongue
  is a fleeting vapor and a snare of death (Prov. 21:6).

The wisdom literature also recognizes that the simple pursuit of wealth for wealth's sake was not a valid or noble pursuit—that wealth is fleeting and therefore untrustworthy in the long run as a source of true satisfaction:

Do not toil to acquire wealth;
  be wise enough to desist.
When your eyes light upon it, it is gone;
  for suddenly it takes to itself wings,
  flying like an eagle toward heaven (Prov. 23:4–5).

He who tills his land will have plenty of bread,
  but he who follows worthless pursuits will have plenty of poverty.
A faithful man will abound with blessings,
  but he who *hastens to be rich* will not go unpunished (Prov.
  28:19–20, emphasis mine).

That last passage in Proverbs sums up the Old Testament teaching on wealth. Wealth is a blessing when it is a reward from the Lord. It should be enjoyed when it is the result of diligence and responsibility and obedience. But it is a *secondary good* that should not be made a *primary good*.

In the Old Testament, we learn God wanted his people to have an abundance of this world's goods, but for the right reasons—as a result of righteous living, not as a result of thievery or a short-circuit approach that made acquiring wealth a primary pursuit apart from obedience to God.

In the New Testament, there is a definite modification in the emphasis on riches—particularly in terms of money or worldly goods. In the Gospels there are numerous verses that speak of the ways riches can hinder a right relationship with God (Matt. 19:23–24; Mark 10:23–25; Luke 18:24–25; Luke 6:24; Luke 12:16 ff.). And Paul warns directly in 1 Timothy that "people who want to get rich fall into temptation and a trap and into many foolish and harmful desires that plunge men into ruin and destruction" (6:9). He cautions church leaders,

> Command those who are rich in this present world not to be arrogant nor to put their hope in wealth, which is so uncertain, but to put their hope in God, who richly provides us with everything for our enjoyment. Command them to do good, to be rich in good deeds, and to be generous and willing to share (vv. 17–18).

But virtually all of these negative New Testament comments can be subsumed under the topic of *misusing* riches or putting too much store in them—not merely possessing them. And the New Testament also shows some wealthy people in a positive light. The parabolic rich man who pardoned his wasteful manager in Luke 16:1–15 is presented as an enlightened pagan at worst. Joseph of Arimathea, a man of substance, is shown using his wealth in a selfless way—giving his own tomb to the crucified Lord (Matt. 27:57). And the loving father in the parable of the Prodigal Son is obviously a man of some means!

When material riches are mentioned in a positive sense, it is almost always in terms of the stewardship or right use of them— as in 2 Corinthians 9:11, where Paul writes, "You will be made rich in every way so that you can be generous on every occasion, and through us your generosity will result in thanksgiving to God" (NIV).

Perhaps the clearest teaching of Christ about the legitimacy of abundance and the necessity of being a steward, whatever wealth one possesses, is his repeated enigmatic teaching, "Whoever has will be given more, and he will have an abundance. Whoever does not have, even what he has will be taken from him" (Matt. 13:12, NIV; also in Matt. 25:29).

So also Jesus says in Luke 16:9, "I tell you, use worldly wealth to gain friends for yourselves, so that when it is gone, you will be welcomed into eternal dwellings." And in verse 11 we find one of Jesus' teachings that presupposes that there is an appropriate kind of riches in his saying, "So if you have not been trustworthy in handling worldly wealth, who will trust you with true riches?" (NIV).

The New Testament, therefore, does not contradict the Old Testament teachings on wealth, but adds strong warnings on the misuse of riches and the powerful trap that exists for those who have an inordinate concern for financial gain.

In addition, significantly, neither the Old nor New Testament teaches any kind of automatic correlation between wealth (or the lack of it) and virtue or value to God. To easily assume that one person's wealth is necessarily a reward for being good or another's poverty is punishment for lack of virtue simply is not valid— although the people of Jesus' day had begun to read it like that.

So, when we say God wants you to be rich, we are *not necessarily* saying he wants your bankroll to be fat—although we are not saying he wants it to be thin, either. The clear message of the Old and New Testament about material wealth is that, whatever your financial resources, they should be used *only for the right purposes and result only from the right kind of moves.* Any material wealth you possess must be acquired only in the context of your unique obedience to him—not as a consequence of your taking off on a tangent and making money your god, and certainly not your being willing to sacrifice your soul or your family's soul in the unfettered pursuit of wealth alone!

Be well aware of wealth's potency and its risk. This is the repeated message of the New Testament. Money is not bad in and of itself, unless it becomes a god and you find yourself bending your life to its demands. Like all potent commodities, it is risky—and it may be that many of us cannot be trusted even to be in the same room with such risky realities. Perhaps that is why many of us find that our financial abundance is rather minimal!

Wealth means a variety of things to different people. To some it represents security for their family and their old age, and their approach is to store it away prudently like squirrels stashing nuts. For others, money means power and prestige and is evidenced by conspicuous consumption—flashy car, clothes, house, or whatever is the fashion of the moment. For still others, wealth represents social status; it allows them to join the right clubs and be seen with the right people. Or it can be used as a substitute for love and relationships—used to "buy" other people's loyalty and affection.

But then there are those for whom money means blessings poured out by God—to be used, enjoyed, and invested with good stewardship. These people see their material wealth as an opportunity to accomplish things for others—family, friends, people in need—and to help further God's kingdom on earth.

As you can see, the problem with wealth is not in the riches themselves, but rather in the *motives* for pursuing, using, storing, and passing it along.

So, is it wrong to pursue wealth? That depends. Why are you pursuing it? And what will you do with it when you get it? If you chase it for the wrong purposes, it is clearly harmful, but for the right purposes and with the right motives it could be OK. But you need also to keep in mind a parallel truth of the New Testament: It is also OK to be poor—once again, if you use that state to be truly dependent on God. Many of the poor are true saints: ". . . Has not God chosen those who are poor in the eyes of the world to be rich in faith and to inherit the kingdom he promised those who love him?" (James 2:5).

In Genesis 12 we read that Abraham was blessed—but that he was *blessed to be a blessing*. Wealth can be righteous when it is used to be a blessing to others. The danger here is that you can really do a number on yourself and end up surrounding yourself with pious platitudes about how that's exactly what you plan to do with God's riches—but, when it comes to the bottom line, you end up using it in the style of the selfish, pagan world around us. Maybe that's why God doesn't entrust wealth to some of us; he knows we couldn't handle it!

=== *SUMMARY* ===

The confident and affable life is one in which you are fully aware of and grateful for the abundant riches God has given you—and are using those riches as a good steward of God's goodness. The affable life is one that is abundant in contentment with whatever level of riches God has entrusted to you and that glories in the contentment of God's wealth. You are abundant in variety as you include a diversity of experiences in your life. Take a walk, invite others into your home and your life. Reach out and meet new people, try new activities, do something for others. Plan a trip, set a goal, hang a light in your tunnel. Living an affable and confident life also means taking care of your body, mind, soul, and spirit through regular disciplines. And it means using whatever material wealth we have to enhance the lives of others and bring honor to God—not pursuing wealth as if it were a god.

You Need to Be More 6
Clarified Than Your Butter

Every good chef knows that butter tastes better than any other fat for frying. But there is a problem with butter—it burns before it reaches the high temperatures necessary for frying. And so a chef learns to melt the butter and let the solid matter settle to the bottom. Then he can pour off the clear, golden liquid at the top —the "clarified" butter—and use it for his fried recipes, because clarified butter has a much higher burning point.

If you want to live confidently and affably, your life needs to go through a clarifying process, too. Clarifying involves letting the things of lesser importance settle out so you can concentrate on the more important substance—your true goals, needs, and high priorities. To put it another way, you need to get rid of fuzziness in your life—clear up the muddy areas—and settle in on who you are and where you are going.

Fuzziness in our thoughts and goals is one of the greatest enemies of a satisfying and confident life. I have counseled with many people who are not really sure who they are, where they are going, what is important to them, or who is important to them. Their lives are confused, and this is not surprising, since there are many forces in our culture that continually muddy the waters.

═══ THE MUDDYING FORCES ═══

OPTION PROLIFERATION

First, there is the ever-expanding number of options. In his landmark book, *Future Shock*, Alvin Toffler pointed out the increasing problem of having too many choices. This is true for most of us, whether we are standing in the breakfast cereal aisle in the supermarket, overwhelmed with a veritable cornucopia of brand names, sizes, and colors (from Fruit Loops to Granola) or standing in a car lot trying to decide about size, color, style, mileage, and status. (Toffler reports that the possible option combinations on a Ford Thunderbird totals some twenty-five million!) How can one choose well in the midst of such a dazzling array of possibilities?

Added to this is the fact that we are continuously deluged by sledge-hammer media entreaties on behalf of a plethora of brand names. Try as we might, it's difficult to deaden the staccato yammering of the ubiquitous hucksters who push, shove, and beg. Buy this! Consider this! And Hurry, Hurry, Hurry—this may be your last chance. . . .

The same is true even of the Christian world. In simpler days, in a small rural town, one's religious choices included a modest few clear-cut alternatives—where I grew up, Baptist, Methodist or Roman Catholic Churches were the religious options. Now the variety of Christian expressions are before us on television, radio, rallies, periodicals, books, conferences. Billy Graham, Oral Roberts, Campus Crusade for Christ, Inter-Varsity, Youth For Christ, Gothard's Basic Youth Conflicts, and many others increasingly beg for our loyalty, funds, time, and energy.

The sensitive and responsible Christian who wants to be a responsible steward of his life sees appeal after appeal in the mail from missionary organizations, orphanages, relief organizations —all worthy, all needy. There are myriad possibilities for spiritual enrichment—travel to the Holy Land, support an orphan, help distribute religious literature.

And there has been a huge proliferation of the religious media that bring these pleas into the home. There are Christian book clubs, music clubs, record and tape clubs. Religious bookstores are burgeoning and are filled with everything from Bible translations to Scripture plaques and "Christian" nightlights.

In large suburban churches, there is an increasing expansion of opportunities for fellowship and mission: child care, counseling, teaching, adult studies, social action, small covenant group fellowship, prayer circles, retreat ministries, sponsoring of children and youth programs. And all of these are in addition to the traditional committees, commissions, or boards which never seem to die. Did you ever notice that in most church programs more and more is added—but virtually nothing is taken away to make room for the new additions?

MISINFORMED EGALITARIANISM

In my mind, another prime culprit in the confusion so many of us suffer is *misinformed egalitarianism*. Part of our American heritage is a virtue that can become a vice—in allowing for democracy and equality, we tend to be suckered into what I like to call "the strawberry-manure fallacy."

Here's what I mean: If a farmer has a pile of manure with which to fertilize his strawberries, he doesn't leave it all piled up on one plant or one area; he spreads it around equally to get the best effect. And that's a good idea for strawberries. But this equal-spread theory is popularly applied to many other pursuits because it is safe and sounds "fair," and it protects people from making hard, selective decisions. The trouble is that what works for strawberries isn't necessarily the best policy in other areas—such as life management.

Military strategy has long recognized the inadequacy of the strawberry-manure approach in planning strategy. You rarely find a great battle that has been won by simply pressing forward on all fronts, keeping all the division commanders happy by giving them each an equal opportunity to share in the victory. No! The genius of military victory is to gather your strength and focus it strategically against a point of weakness in the enemy's line, destroying the enemy by pitting strength against weakness. This means making hard decisions, the kind of decisions that General Dwight Eisenhower constantly faced in the European war when dealing with the various competing strategies proposed by Generals Montgomery, Bradley, Patton, and so forth.

I have found that the strawberry-manure approach is especially widespread in Christian circles. For example, in our great desire to be generous-minded, loving, and egalitarian in a Christian sense, we tend to spread our mission giving across the board, rather than making the hard decision that one particular effort is really of more strategic value than another and giving to that more valuable effort the dollars that will bring it to fruition.

How does this particular fallacy work out in our daily lives? We tend to belong to too many good organizations and spread ourselves too thin, rather than making hard choices and giving ourselves more strategically to a limited number of causes. Or we buy a houseful of cheap furniture to cover all the rooms rather than buying fewer pieces of better furniture that will retain their value and usefulness for a long time. Or, we try to be good friends with too broad a group of people and end without having enough time to build deep and important relationships with any of them.

If a traveler tries to cover too many places—see too many cities, drive too many miles—the whole trip becomes a wearying blur; as the old movie title put it, *If It's Tuesday, This Must Be Belgium*. How much better to pick two or three important places and see them in a leisurely and thorough fashion! And the same is true of almost any aspect of our lives. Fuzziness is perpetuated by refusing to make hard priority decisions.

THE AREAS THAT NEED CLARIFYING

What are the fuzzy areas in our lives that could benefit from the clarifying process? And how do we go about clarifying those important areas?

The wisdom literature of the Old Testament—Psalms, Proverbs, and Ecclesiastes—can be helpful in answering these questions because these Books put a lot of emphasis on gaining understanding or insight. According to these books, many things are important to understand: the nature of God and man, the way things really are in human society, where things are going to end up—and much more.

One of the most enigmatic of all the puzzles that need to be understood is ourselves. We study ourselves to learn about others; we study others to learn about ourselves. And that is the place to start when it comes to clarifying our lives. Baruch Spinoza had this in mind when he said, "I have tried sedulously not to laugh at the acts of man, nor to lament them, nor to detest them, but to understand them." And this theme is also clearly set forth in Proverbs:

> The beginning of wisdom is this: Get wisdom,
>   and whatever you get, get insight.
> Prize her highly, and she will exalt you;
>   she will honor you if you embrace her.
> She will place on your head a fair garland;
>   she will bestow on you a beautiful crown (4:7–9).

CLARIFYING WHAT WORKS (EXERCISE 1)

Some of the most helpful insights in the wisdom literature have to do with what really "works" in life. Since ancient times, people have tried all kinds of approaches to life—and they have found that some of these approaches work and some don't.

Over the centuries, this experience of daily life was distilled into pithy and terse sayings which were polished, refined, and passed along as poetic couplets, aphorisms, dictums, or maxims. Sometimes these sayings crossed borders and were shared across cultural and national lines. Thus we find in the Old Testament sayings that were also found in similar writings in other Near East cultures. In them we find a summary of centuries of experience. Here are some of them in my own paraphrase:

Keep your mouth shut and you'll avoid a great deal of problems (Prov. 10:19)

Don't co-sign a note, or you may get taken to the cleaners (Proverbs 6:1–5).

Don't pull practical jokes (Prov. 26:18–19).

Don't toot your own horn (Prov. 27:2).

Don't make a pest of yourself by going to your neighbor's house too much (Prov. 25:17).

In clarifying our lives, we need not only to profit from such tested wisdom of the past, but also to examine the patterns of our lives today and ask ourselves some searching questions about the things that occupy our time, our energy, our enthusiasm, and our money. We need to apply to all our pursuits that key question, *does it work?*

It is easy to fall into lifestyle patterns without giving them careful thought. While I was in college, I worked in a parking garage in downtown Seattle. One of the fellows I worked with was named Les. He had been married several times, was paying alimony to more than one wife, and was having a tough time in his current marriage. He was a hard worker and fairly steady, but he did do a good deal of after-hours drinking that occasionally interfered with his work. Les would get off work about four in the afternoon and immediately head for the bar up the street. He would sit there and drink until about nine or ten before he went home. Sometimes he wouldn't show up on the job the next morning. So periodically Les would get fired, but then the boss would relent and take him back.

Les and I had a pretty good relationship and sometimes he would open up to me—share something of his agonies and woes. So I asked him one day about his life pattern. I didn't understand how he was solving any of his problems in the bar.

I asked him, "How's it working?"

He replied, "It ain't working at all."

"Then why don't you change it?"

"I don't know any other way to handle the pain. Even though it isn't working, it's less painful than any other alternative I've tried—like not drinking, or going straight home."

One of the frequent problems people face in our day and age is not knowing anything that really works well, not having an understanding of effective lifestyle options.

In counseling people who are facing painful emotional problems, I am regularly confronted with those who feel they have painted themselves into a corner. They don't have a clue about how to come up with hopeful alternatives that actually pay off. I seek to help them clarify some good alternatives they hadn't thought of or tried.

Remember Lucy's constant unrequited love for Schroeder in "Peanuts"? As she constantly tries to initiate a romance with this child prodigy, she usually drapes herself over his tiny grand piano while he is practicing.

One day Schroeder is playing and Lucy says, "I've decided something. . . . You and I are through!"

Schroeder looks up and responds, "How can we be through? We never even started!" and he returns immediately to his piano playing, ignoring her completely.

In the last frame, Lucy turns around to think about this and concludes, "That didn't even come close to working!"

As an aid to pinpointing what works in your life, try this exercise. Take a blank sheet of paper and rule it off as in Exercise 1. List some of the activities that occupy your time, money, energy, and talents. Then estimate what the "payoff" is for that activity (write it as a percentage). Jot down the results of the activity in terms of its effect on your life (how it makes you feel, how it affects others). Then, based on the payoff and results you figured, write a conclusion about whether you should do more or less of that activity.

Exercise 1
DETERMINING WHAT WORKS
(*Sample*)

Activity	Payoff	Results of Doing Activity	Conclusion
Daily walk	95%	I almost always feel good for having one—in fact, I've never regretted taking a walk.	Do more
Watching TV	20%	Usually feel like I have wasted my time—I need to pick programs more selectively.	Do less
Attending church	80%	Feel guilty if I don't go. Sometimes sermon is good. Enjoy seeing my friends—I should talk to more people at coffee hour. It would be better if I took more initiative in introducing myself to new people.	Do more
Reading	65%	Need to be more selective. Some is a real waste; some is helpful.	Do more
Spending time with daughter	80%	Pays off when I do it —better relationship.	Do more
Communi-cation with wife	85%	Atmosphere improves when I work at this—pays off.	Do more
Hanging around poolroom	65%	Used to be better—lots of time I go home disappointed. The old gang is getting a bit threadbare.	Do less!
Talking to broker	50%	Depends on market. Some-times I have a headache after talking with him.	Need to rethink
Working in garden	30%	Keeps wife happy but I hate it. I get tired and I find it boring.	Consider hiring a gardener
Occasional ski trips	95%	When I do it I feel great about it.	Maybe one or two more per year
Tennis	65%	Know it is good for me.	Should do more
Bible study	85%	Helps me get perspective. I get guidance.	Do more

You pick your own topics. You set your own payoff scale. And you can mix both serious and trivial activities—whatever things you regularly do as a part of your lifestyle. The purpose of this is simply to raise your awareness level regarding the things you do and whether these things pay off for you. Do they warrant a place in your life? Should you do more or less of them?

You might also want to list some things you don't now do but would like to do—learning needlepoint, studying Esperanto, memorizing Scripture. Ask yourself about these possible activities, "What kind of payoff would they bring? What would be their results?"

CLARIFYING WHO IS IMPORTANT TO YOU (EXERCISE 2)

When I have taught life-management seminars, one of the first exercises I have asked people to do involves clarifying *who* is important to them. I ask them to draw a series of concentric circles (about three of them) and write in the rings the names of the key people in their lives—the most valued people in the inner ring, the less valued people in the second ring, and those at the least level of importance in the outer ring. It's not as easy as it sounds!

Exercise 2
EVALUATING THE
PEOPLE IN YOUR LIFE
(*Sample*)

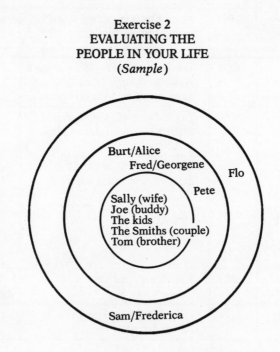

Burt/Alice
Fred/Georgene
Flo
Pete
Sally (wife)
Joe (buddy)
The kids
The Smiths (couple)
Tom (brother)
Sam/Frederica

I usually ask married couples to make this list separately and not to share it with their mate, because some people are not ready to accept their mate's list of people-priorities.

John and Karla, for instance, went home from a seminar and had a real rip-roaring argument over who the husband had put in his "inner circle"—in particular his senior partner; he was loyal to his boss. Karla didn't care much for the partner due to their difference in lifestyles and value systems. And so they went round and round. In the end the exercise was valuable, for they did end up clarifying some things about their marital relationship, but it was touch and go for awhile!

The point of this clarification procedure is not primarily to interact with another person (such as your spouse) about your values, but to think seriously about *your own* values as indicated by who is important to you and why. Knowing that you are going to share this information with someone else—especially someone close to you—might inhibit you and keep you from being completely candid with yourself.

Harmonizing Goals and People. But what is the long-range purpose of all this? *The purpose is to prepare you to set up goals that will be in harmony with your deeper values.* (We'll look at goal setting in more detail in the next chapter.) And some of our deepest values come from the people we cherish most. There may not be much point in piling up money, for example, if all the people who are really important to you could care less about your money and would rather have your time and your attention!

A popular phrase in our culture is "getting it all together"—and this is an important notion when it comes to clarifying your life. It involves having your cherished people and your most basic goals in harmony, so that you can pursue your goals without running into continual conflicts with those you care about.

Interpersonal conflict often results when people have fuzzy notions about who and what is really important to them—they have what is known as a values conflict or dysfunction. They start off pursuing a goal, and then find not only that they are not supported by those close to them, but that their goal is in basic conflict with those whom they care most about.

An important resource in moving toward goals is the continued emotional support of people who will cheer you on, who will affirm you when it gets bleak. It is a fact of life that almost everyone needs encouragement.

The cheers of a hometown crowd make a discernible difference in a basketball or football game. Some oddsmakers say that a home-court advantage in a major basketball game can be as much as fifteen points! A close supportive group can give you measurable boosts in challenge, affirmation, guidance, and direction. In order to accomplish important goals, we need people who are committed to us and on our side. It follows that clarification of who *is* important to you can be most strategic.

What happens if you find that your "inner circle" people are not the ones who will truly support you in your pursuit of your high priorities? Major disharmony between your goals and the people closest to you might mean one of several things to you.

It could mean that you should *rethink* your declared goals. You may be kidding yourself. Perhaps your choice of people close to you reveals more about you than your stated goals.

Or it may be that you need to sit down and *communicate* with those who are close to you. Perhaps your spouse or children are not supportive of your goals, and you need to talk with them about the fact that you have some goals that are not congruent with their expectations. Often, when the cards are laid upon the table, some sort of "I win, You win" arrangement can be worked out—a trade-off that allows your "inner circle" to get some things they need from you and in turn to give you support toward your goals.

Still another possibility is to search your "outer circles" for some people who might encourage you in meeting your goals. If you find them, perhaps you can work them into your inner friendship circle. (Obviously, some care would be indicated here. It wouldn't really be a good idea to cultivate a close friendship just to encourage you in a goal your wife or husband is dead set against!)

All of which is to say that if you are going to launch into a program of significant self-improvement and work toward building a more confident and affable life, you need to know how this is going to be received by the people who are closest and dearest to you. When we make changes in our lives, we need to keep a very clear perception of the realities—and the people close to us are very much a part of these realities.

Would You Die for Me? On one episode of the TV show, *All in the Family,* Gloria came home with a bee in her bonnet, questioning how important she was to her husband, Michael. Although she brought the subject up precipitously and at the wrong time, she had a valid concern about her place in his changing life. He was working on his M.A. while she only had a high-school diploma and was working as a clerk in a store. It had dawned on her that as he became more educated, he might lose interest in her. She needed reassurance that she still held a significant place in his life.

The way Gloria brought the subject up to Michael was to ask him very abruptly, "Would you die for me?" And of course, they were off to the races—a fight ensued. But although Gloria's question was extreme—and difficult to answer—it was not totally off target. Asking ourselves, "Who would I be willing to die for?" can be a very significant way of asking, "Who is important to me? How important? How valuable?"

There are other questions we can ask ourselves that can help us discriminate about how much we value other people. Who would you *loan* five thousand dollars to—or *give* five hundred dollars? Who would you borrow money from? Who would you share your home with? Your room? And who would you spend a day off or a two-week vacation with?

There is an almost infinite number of questions that could be posed. And they are all ways of emphasizing that people do not all mean the same to us. Some might object that such questions are so hypothetical that they don't mean much. But we all do make both crucial and trivial distinctions among people. Some people we offer a ride; others we don't. Some people we seek out; others we avoid. Some people could ask us for aid and we would readily go out of our way to help them; others we quickly refer to agencies or share with them one of our handy, but very legitimate, excuses.

(Some girls in a college dorm had the problem of what to do when they wanted to turn down a date from someone they didn't want to go out with. To solve the problem, one of them wrote a list of ten handy excuses and tacked them up next to the phone in the hall. It worked pretty well except for the time one girl got flustered and said to the earnest caller, "I'd love to go out with you, Tom, but I can't—because of Number Seven.")

Who is really important to you? And *how* do *you* decide? A confident and affable relationship with life requires some pretty clear answers to those questions.

CLARIFICATION OF VALUES AND PRINCIPLES (EXERCISE 3)

It is important in the clarification process to understand what values are vital to you. In order to get the varied dynamics of your life pushing in one direction, you need to comprehend the

Exercise 3
SAMPLE VALUES

A satisfying family life
A nice home
Opportunity to travel
Financial security
Good health for myself
Peace with God
An attractive mate
A satisfying vocation
Healthy children
A satisfying sex life
A sense of accomplishment
To be my own boss

To be surrounded by a circle
of close friends
To rise to a position of power
in a large company
To discover a cure for cancer
To live to age ninety-five
To live close to children and
grandchildren
To write the great American novel
Self-achievement
Assurance of eternal life

YOUR VALUES

Value	Why Important	Rank
1.		
2.		
3.		
4.		
5.		
6.		

underlying value system you have lodged deeply in your psyche. This can be done in a variety of ways. Here is an exercise to help you:

Listed in the table for Exercise 3 are twenty different abstract and particular values that some people say are important to them. They are merely initial suggestions—you can add your choices to the side of the list.

From the sample list and your own additions, pick out six values that seem particularly strategic to you. Write them in the blanks below the sample list. (To get started, it might be helpful to cross off the ten or more that seem to you the least important.) Then, next to each one, jot down a brief sentence as to why it is important to you. (You will probably find there is a good deal of overlapping, with similar reasons for several values.) Finally, rank those six according to how important they are to you and write the corresponding number from one to six in the blanks to the right. (You can do all this on a separate sheet of paper if you prefer.)

Once at an organizational development conference I attended, we went through this exercise—except we were asked to rank all twenty of the suggestions listed in exercise 3. Then we shared our lists with one another in small groups, interpreting and explaining our choices. One member of our group, a man named Harry, ranked "self-achievement" down near the tail end of his list—either seventeenth or eighteenth. And he made a noble-sounding speech about how he really wasn't "achievement oriented."

The next day, however, we were put through a similar exercise having to do with our daily work. We were asked to make a list of all the various projects or activities we had been involved with in the previous few weeks. Then we were asked to rank those activities according to what they meant to us in terms of satisfaction and meaning. After we had identified the projects that were most meaningful to us in our work, we were asked to examine the dynamics of *why* those particular activities were so meaningful to us.

We were then instructed to retrieve our values list from the previous day. And as Harry looked first at his values list, then at his project list, he had one of those amazing "Aha" moments. He said, "Wow, I've been kidding myself. Yesterday I put self-achievement way down at the bottom and even made a speech about how unimportant it was to me. But I just noticed that in all the work projects that bring me enjoyment and fulfillment, the really satisfying element is the sense of personal self-achievement that comes from the project."

Here is a good example of what can happen when we examine our values closely. In our conscious minds we may carry one notion about what is important to us—perhaps a notion we see as noble and presentable to others. But as a matter of fact, the things that we really are doing and enjoying behind the scenes may reveal another value system—one that may be hidden even from our own view.

The result, of course, is fuzziness in our value system. And the plain truth is that we are not going to be focused in our lives nor be able to go after that which is important to us until we discover precisely what our value system really looks like.

If you previously did Exercise 1, compare the values list you just made in Exercise 3 with the list of activities from Exercise 1. Are the two lists congruent? How do they relate? Do you have your values together so that you really are functioning in a harmonious way within yourself?

CLARIFICATION OF HIGHLY SIGNIFICANT ACTIVITIES (EXERCISE 4)

Sidney Simon, Leland Howe, and Howard Kirschenbaum, in their helpful book, *Values Clarification,** suggest a stimulating exercise that I have used many times with small groups as a discussion starter. It is very helpful in shedding light on the nuts and bolts of our activities.

To do the exercise, first take a blank sheet of paper ruled off as in the example and list right off the top of your head twenty activities you *like* to engage in. (You can use those from Exercise 1 over again or come up with a brand-new list.)

The activities can be profound, trivial, occasional, or regular. As quickly as they come to your mind, jot them down without editing. What do you like to do? How do you like to spend your time? Hike? Pray? Go to restaurants? Read books? Go for a walk? Work on your computer? Visit your neighbor? Listen to opera on your CD player? Read the Bible? Play bridge? Plan a party? Write them down.

After you have completed the list, you begin the evaluation stage. In the first column (A), there is a dollar sign. Go down the list and note with a dollar sign each one of these activities that requires more than ten dollars. A very interesting thing takes place when this is done in a group. Some people find that virtually

*(New York: Hart Publishing, 1972).

Exercise 4
EVALUATING YOUR ACTIVITIES

Name of Activity	A ($)	B (A/P)	C (O/N)
1.			
2.			
3.			
4.			
5.			
6.			
7.			
8.			
9.			
10.			
11.			
12.			
13.			
14.			
15.			
16.			
17.			
18.			
19.			
20.			

none of their choices cost more than ten dollars, that most of the things they like to do are "freebies"—such as taking a walk, visiting the library, calling on neighbors, whittling a stick. Others discover that a great number of their chosen activities cost money —dining out, going to a movie, buying new clothes, or flying to Bermuda.

Now, in column B, mark a "P" for those things you would normally do with another person and an "A" for those you would normally do alone. If the activity could be done either way (alone or with another person), mark it "A/P." Then look at your completed column. What does it say about you? Are you basically a loner or a "people person"—or a little of both?

I think you have the idea by now. For column C, you go through your list again, this time marking a "O" if the activity is one you would have been doing five years ago—an *old*, established pattern—and an "N" if it is a relatively *new* activity for you. Once more, look at the pattern. What does it reveal about your interest in and ability to change?

Finally, for each column ask yourself, "What does this pattern say about the kinds of things I value?" Write a sentence for each one of these columns in which you interpret the patterns that emerge. (Read Simon, Howe, and Kirschenbaum's book, *Values Clarification*, for a great number of such exercises for clarifying your life.)

If we are the kinds of people who are growing in our self-awareness about who we are, we are going to be able to move smartly toward an affable and confident life.

CLARIFICATION OF TIME (EXERCISE 5)

Most of us let time slip through our fingers without even being certain where our time goes. One way to enrich your life is to make a point of setting aside more time for your high-priority activities. Learn to use your time and make it work for you.

A good way to begin the time clarification process is to make a careful two-week assessment of the way you are currently using your time. Such an assessment need not be fussy or nit-picking to be of help—although it does involve a certain amount of work.

Make up your chart for keeping track of your time (or use the chart printed here) and keep close tabs on yourself for a couple of weeks. Be careful to choose a couple of weeks that are fairly typical of your time; try not to pick the busiest time of the year, or the slackest, or a week when you are off at a convention.

Before you start, decide on the major categories you will keep track of and set up a system for noting which category a recording activity falls in. On the next page are some suggestions for codes you could use on the time chart.

As you finish up each day, sum up the total number of hours spent in each kind of activity. (Some rounding off is OK—but it goes without saying that your chart will be only as valid as your recording is accurate.) After the two-week period, total up the

SL	Sleep (Amount and patterns, naps)
TR	Travel to and from work
WK	Work itself
ET	Eating (including chatting around the table)
PC	Personal care (bathing, beauty treatment, hair cuts, brushing teeth, exercise)
GO	Goofing off, entertainment, talking on the phone, lying around, watching TV
PB	Personal business (writing checks, balancing your checkbook, raking the yard, puttering around the house, unplugging the stopped-up toilet)
SO	Service to others, community or church volunteer work
FL	Fellowship, shooting the bull with buddies
PL	Planning
WO	Worship, Bible study, church fellowship activities
____	(fill in your own)
____	
____	

daily amounts and take a careful look at the overall pattern. If you are like most people who have done this for the first time you are going to find it a most enlightening experience.

(It might also be very interesting to ask two or three other people whom you know pretty well and whose schedules are similar to yours to do this project at the same time you do it. Compare notes, and discuss the significance of your results.)

After completing your two-week assessment period, move to the next step, which is to ask yourself some questions. What does your chart say about the way you are using your time? Where can you pick up some extra time to be used in pursuits that are important to you? Where are you using time in activities that are not paying off?

Most important is the question, "Of all of these activities that I am doing—which are actually moving me toward what I want to achieve in my life?" How much time am I *actually* devoting to making those goals happen? (In chapter 7, we will discuss goal

Exercise 5
TIME USE CLARIFICATION

	Monday	Tuesday	Wednesday	Thursday	Friday	Saturday	Sunday
6:00AM							
6:30AM							
7:00AM							
7:30AM							
8:00AM							
8:30AM							
9:00AM							
10:00AM							
10:30AM							
11:00AM							
11:30AM							
NOON							
12:30PM							
1:00PM							
1:30PM							
2:00PM							
2:30PM							
3:00PM							
3:30PM							
4:00PM							
4:30PM							
5:00PM							
5:30PM							
6:00PM							
6:30PM							
7:00PM							
7:30PM							
8:00PM							
8:30PM							
9:00PM							
9:30PM							
10:00PM							
10:30PM							
11:00PM							
11:30PM							
MIDNITE							

setting in some detail.) Most of us tend to dribble our lives away on things that are handy, convenient, and trivial, so that we have no time left for the things that we say and believe are most important to us.

To help you assess your time use, look at your final list of time allotments with the following standard in mind: Most time use will tend to fall in one of four categories: (1) Time spent on high aspirations; (2) time spent on necessities; (3) regeneration time; and (4) wasted time.

That may sound like a rather narrow set of evaluation categories—and it may tend to force you to put a lot of things under category four. But this is intentional, because an important part of time clarification is becoming aware of how much time we tend to waste.

Let's consider these four categories in more detail:

Time Spent on High Aspirations. This is the category we need deliberately to set aside time for—because this is what we say we are really here for, designed to do.

Time Spent on Necessities. This category includes the activities we must carry out simply to live—and which most likely take up a great amount of time. Necessities would include eating, sleeping, work, personal care, clothing maintenance, and so on. This category may not fill any needs but to provide food and shelter, but clearly food and shelter are high priorities!

Regeneration Time. We also need time to rest, to worship God, to relax, to be entertained, to serve, to be diverted with a change of pace. All of these things represent our need for regeneration, getting our batteries recharged, our spirits lifted, our life brought back in focus. Regeneration time is not wasted time—although there may be a temptation to waste time by lingering too long in a regenerative activity!

Waste. Many people tend to spend too much time in one or more of the "regenerative" activities until these activities lose their restorative power and simply become a waste of time.

Let me illustrate. Tom happens to like to watch a few specific television programs, usually those that are on after ten in the evening. Since his work takes him out a number of nights a week and he often comes home keyed up, he finds that watching a show or two helps him relax and wind down. Up to a certain number of nights and a certain number of minutes, that kind of television watching is regenerative for him. But if inertia sets in and he continues to sit in front of that television for several hours, night after night, his television watching can cease to be regenerative and has crossed over the line into simply a time-waster.

Another example: Sarah works hard at cleaning and ironing and needs a break, so she goes next door to her girlfriend's house for a cup of coffee—or she gives someone a call. That's good; we all can profit from an occasional break. But when the visit goes on and on—or the phone call lasts an hour—regenerative time has turned into wasted time.

Time clarification is that process where we take an informed and hard look at our schedule *as it is actually lived*, and we make some judgments and decisions based upon the discovery that there are a number of time slots where we can turn wasted time into time spent on the pursuit of our high-priority goals.

Now, I am not suggesting that you eliminate all entertainment, or goofing off, or coffee breaks, or television from your life—you may choose to eliminate any activity for a time to make sure you are in control and that a bad habit is not running your schedule. The need for regeneration is real, and each one of us needs a certain amount of easy spaces in our schedule. If Jack doesn't get some play he can indeed become a dull boy—as well as ineffective and irritable. What I am suggesting is that, rather that simply *drifting* unconsciously into time-use patterns, we get in *control of our time* and make it an ally.

Before we leave this matter of time clarification, I would like to add an observation on the variations in the quality of time. Time is not equal. Each of us has a kind of natural biological rhythm that makes some times more suitable for productive work than others. Some people are morning bloomers. Others are night people. And there are a million gradations in between.

Take a moment just now to think about the various times of the day, the week, the month, the year. Ask yourself some hard questions about what times are the *best* ones and which are the *least effective* for you. How would you grade the various times of day?

Here's the way one person might grade the time in their day:

6:00–9:30 A.M.   Early morning—worst level (#5).
Totally involved in coming back to
sentient life. Start out the day at the
Early Neanderthal stage of life with
inaudible grunts.

9:30 A.M.–noon	Late morning—tied for best level (#1). Functioning well and with enthusiasm.
Noon–1:00 P.M.	Lunch—pretty good (#2) level. Tied for second. Eating enhances disposition.
1–3:00 P.M.	Early afternoon—fair to middling, but not too hot (#3) level. Busy digesting lunch.
3:00–5:00 P.M.	Late afternoon—next to the worst level (#4). Would really prefer to take a nap.
5:00–7:00 P.M.	Travel and transition—back to home, family, supper, reserved for family, not available—flaked out on couch awaiting supper, reading paper. Time out.
7:00–9:00 P.M.	Early evening—things starting to look better; all in all, pretty good. #2 level.
9:00 P.M.–midnight or 2:00 A.M.	Late evening—velvet hours, no interrupting phone calls. Outstanding time of day—tied for #1.

The same person might clarify his weekly schedule this way:

Monday	The week usually starts tough, but gets better every day.
Tuesday/Wednesday	Hardest days of the week. Tend to most of detail, paper shuffling, staff conferences, coordinating around office, writing memos, answering phone calls. Usually long days— ending late at night either with a class or a committee meeting.
Thursday	Getting better, less pressures in office. (Boss busy with other things and is not pestering staff.) Combination paper shuffling and some planning and writing.
Friday	Better yet—number of elective meetings and lunches usually

	scheduled—some study—less paperwork.
Saturday	Day off. Mow the lawn. "Honey Do" list. See Fred next door and chat in his garage. Good day, change of pace. Relax on Saturday night.
Sunday	Busy but excellent—invigorated by teaching, worship, and various family activities.

Your schedule, of course, might look completely different (and should be done in much more detail). But the knowledge you gain about yourself from such a survey can help you plan your time use intelligently by scheduling activities for the times when you can best handle them.

In my job as a pastor, for example, I am involved in a variety of activities. Some are mentally and spiritually demanding and require thought, decision making, and concentration. I would usually only do these things in the late evening or morning. Other things are somewhat mindless and routine (shuffling paper, running errands). They are easy and not demanding. I try to place them in the late afternoon or early evening, when my I.Q. tends to take a sharp dip.

Peter Drucker, in *The Effective Executive*, condemns what he sees as a drift toward mediocrity in American society; he writes that there are certain shifts that will inevitably move us toward the mediocre level. I believe one dimension of this phenomenon in personal life has to do with the qualitative *misuse* of time. "The tyranny of the urgent" (someone else's high priorities) begins to eat up our best time, so that we only have our least effective times available for our high-priority goals.

Controlling our use of time is not easy. It requires discipline and courage—and, most of all, developing the ability to say "No!"—to resist the tyranny of the urgent. But the effort is infinitely worthwhile in learning to live confidently.

Before her passing, the great mystery writer Agatha Christie was asked to give an interview to a writer from *New Yorker* magazine. She declined, and included in her response were the following words:

> I think that people who offer writing to the world, or their paintings or music, have a right to a quiet private life, when they

can meditate and think of interesting ideas they might want to write about. . . . I am now 81 years of age, and I feel, having just published my 81st book, that I am entitled to enjoy the happiness of a quiet life. . . . Sorry if I seem disobliging, but at 81 one does know one's own mind and avoids what one does not like.*

It is my heartfelt wish that we might quickly know our own minds as well, and all of us might arrive at that state—and *well before* we reach age eighty-one!

CLARIFICATION OF ASPIRATIONS

It is important to have aspirations. Sometimes Christians have dismissed aspirations as evidence of humankind's prideful, selfish, sinful nature. Ambition and aspiration are dirty words to some.

But I don't believe aspirations in themselves are either wrong or right; it is the *kind* of aspiration that makes the difference. If one's aspirations are to stomp on people on the way up the ladder of success—then they are contrary to affable living. But if the aspirations are healthy, productive, and positive things that will enable yourself and others, they can be an important motivation for a confident and productive life. They are the kind of aspirations Louisa May Alcott meant when she wrote,

Far away there in the sunshine are my highest aspirations. I may not reach them, but I can look up and see their beauty, believe in them and try to follow them where they lead.†

═══ SUMMARY ═══

An affable relationship with life is more possible when you have a clear view of who and what is important to you—if your life is clarified.

Papillon, imprisoned on Devil's Island, was able to focus singlemindedly on escape and freedom because he cleared his mind and life of extraneous concerns that might fuzz his thinking. Once he had a clear view of what he wanted to accomplish, the way was clear for him to figure out how he might do it.

It is difficult to keep our lives clarified because there are so many options and so many demands that pull us in every direction. To counter this proliferation of confusing options and trends, we need always to be in the process of clarifying what works in

Forbes, 1 June 1976, p. 19.
†*Forbes*, 1 July 1976, p. 108.

life, who is important to us, what our values are, and what activities are particularly significant for us. Keeping an inventory of our time use and becoming aware of our most productive hours and days can help us focus more quality time on our aspirations, necessities, and high-priority goals.

══ FOR FURTHER READING ══

For further help on the subject of time management, I recommend Tony and Robbie Fanning's book, *Get It All Done & Still Be Human: A Time-Management Workshop.** This practical book offers helpful direction for keeping your priorities in order and managing your life.

*(Radnor, PA: Chilton, 1979).

If You're Headed for 7 *Kalamazoo, What Are You Doing on Mexicana Airlines?*

Some years back, a television ad showed a frantic young man on an airplane asking the people around him, one at a time, if the plane went to Miami. He'd found himself on Western Airlines when he wanted to go to Florida, and his assumption was that Western Airlines didn't fly to Miami. He ended up pestering the stewardess, and then finally the pilot came out to assure him that Western Airlines did, indeed, fly to Florida.

Though the young man was portrayed as a bit foolish, his concern was legitimate. If we have a certain "destination"—a goal—in mind, we need to be sure we are pointed in the right direction and on the route that will get us there. Papillon's goal was escape from Devil's Island and freedom. So he made sure he had a confirmed reservation on Lisette Airlines!

THE SPECTRUM OF GOALS

We all have goals. They range from the trivial to the profound and may pertain to any aspect of life. An immediate goal may be to finish a report or take a trip or attend a seminar. A long-range goal may be to travel in every state of the union or send your children to college.

Your goals may be work-related or concerned with any other important part of your life—your family, health, or retirement. At this point they may just be vague ideas about what you'd eventually like to do. But fuzzy or not—they're still goals.

A goal is a specific choice we make about where we are going in life—what we want to do, who we want to become, how we want to live. And we can't live without making choices. Therefore it's impossible not to have goals—your goals are either useful and clear or fuzzy and unhelpful.

═══ USEFUL GOALS ═══

In order to be most useful, goals should be written in nonfuzzy terms, reviewed regularly, and modified as needed. To be more specific, a useful goal is a future state or event (short, intermediate or long-range) you seek to accomplish and which can be measured in time and by performance standards.

This definition is important not only for what it says, but also for what it does *not* say. We are not talking about goals that are fuzzy, subjective, or unmeasurable. A goal is most helpful if you are able to know precisely when and where it has been reached.

My good friend Brett Harns said to me one day at lunch, "My goal is to become a better person." That sounds noble—but how in the world would Brett know whether or not he had reached it? I pressed him further and said, "Well, how would you know whether you were a better person?" He answered, "Well, for one thing, I guess I would feel I was a better person if I quit screaming at my wife so much."

Now, when you add the "Quit Screaming" element, Brett's goal has a performance standard built into it. It is measurable and quantifiable and therefore useful. His goal is to progress from a state of screaming at his wife seven times per week (his current rate) to zero times per week.

A goal should include a time factor: "I want to come to the place (starting today) where I do not scream at my wife for the rest of my life." This is a long-range goal. In order to make it more applicable and useful, the person making the goal should add some intermediate, short-term goals as well: "I have set a short-range goal of not screaming at my wife all week, at which time I will review and renew the program for the next month."

This emphasis on making goals specific, measurable, and time-oriented is not an idle notion. The temptation is always to make goals vague, unmeasurable, and indefinite. When left fuzzy, goals pose no real challenge to us; we need make no progress toward them today, or this week. But when we get serious about goals, we make them specific and measurable. A goal will often begin as a fuzzy idea in our minds, but in order to be truly useful that goal must become increasingly focused.

My friend Sam Henry told me that one of his goals is to travel. I said to Sam, "That's pretty broad. Where to? The South Seas? Across town? Europe? The North Pole? And when? Within two years, four years, or after you retire?"

Questions like that bring a goal into focus. If your goal is travel, what do you want to get out of the travel? The ability to drop the names of "in" places you have visited? If so, you had better start by making a list of the most "in" places, put them in a priority order, and start pricing the tickets. Or maybe you just want to get away from home, your job, your kids, your phone. In that case, perhaps a visit to a resort or hotel in the next town would do the job!

Maybe you want to see certain *kinds* of places. Historical places? If so, which ones? Waterloo? The Cape of Good Hope? The Red Sea? The Lincoln Memorial? Or do you want to see well-known places of natural beauty and grandeur—the Grand Canyon, the Canadian Rockies, Poipu Beach, Victoria Falls?

You will only get enrichment and satisfaction from your goals as you develop them in precise terms that reflect your true inner longings.

Just to get a feel for how the process works, stop now and, in the space provided on the next page, write out three goals that are important to you. Be sure each one is measurable and specific. At this point, don't worry about making these your "life goals" or even your top-priority goals; in the rest of the chapter we will see how to prioritize and clarify goals. Your purpose right now is to practice writing goals in a useful and achievable form.

GOAL #1
(a short-range goal—to be completed in less than a year)

Goal: _____

_____

_____

Reason why important: _____

_____

Today's date: _____ Date to be completed: _____

GOAL #2
(an intermediate goal, completed in one to three years)

Goal: _____

_____

_____

Reason why important: _____

_____

Today's date: _____ Date to be completed: _____

GOAL #3
(a long-range goal—four years or more)

Goal: _____

_____

_____

Reason why important: _____

_____

Today's date: _____ Date to be completed: _____

═══ IN PENCIL WITH AN ERASER ═══

There is one danger in setting goals. When we finally get around to setting them, we tend to think of goals as rigid and unchangeable—almost as if we had written them with a chisel on tablets of stone. Then, when we find that our goals don't materialize exactly as we envisioned, we throw down the tablets and smash them. Then we feel guilty because we are not living up to the divine law we have set for ourselves from our own Mt. Sinai!

Making goals specific and measurable doesn't mean they can never be changed! Quite the opposite! I believe goals should be written in pencil, as tentative and changeable. They may need to be occasionally revised and rewritten—or even discarded altogether.

Goals should be tools to aid us in life, not monsters to intimidate us. Goal setting is a process by which we think creatively about the future, cull out the junk, and then focus more diligently on what's really important to us. But in the process of living with a particular goal, we may discover that we don't really want to pursue it after all.

So don't bronze your goals like your baby shoes—write them down lightly, as in sand, and revise them periodically. Try them on for size, fraternize with them, nudge them around, reshape them, and hopefully, in the process, refine them into something truly helpful. In the words of organizational management guru Ed Dayton of World Vision: "Clear goals, ladies and gentlemen! Clear Goals! Goals that are reviewed regularly to see if they are still viable and discarded if they are not. This must be the foundation."*

To loosen up your thinking a little on the process of goal setting, stop at this point, take a blank sheet of paper, and "brainstorm" some more goal possibilities. Try to keep them measurable and specific, but don't judge them as to whether they're possible or not. Just be sure they're something *you* (not someone else) would like to happen in your life. Here are few suggestions to kick-start the creative-thinking part of your brain:

- The kind of person I'd like to be (Be specific)
- What I'd need to do to be that person
- Places I'd like to go
- Things I'd like to own

Christian Leadership Letter, June 1974.

- Classes/courses of study I'd like to take
- Skills I'd like to acquire
- People I'd like to know better
- Titles or degrees I'd like to acquire
- Books I'd like to read
- Vocational goals
- Financial goals
- A language I'd like to learn
- Things I'd like to accomplish

══ "BE" GOALS AND "DO" GOALS ══

An important distinction can be made between goals that involve the kind of person you want to become and goals that concern the things you want to accomplish.

"BE" GOALS

To develop an affable relationship with life, you need to deal with the vital issue of who you want to become—what kind of character traits you want to develop, or change, or get rid of. This is where our "be" goals come in.

But even "be" goals involve specific actions. For once you have decided you want to be a certain kind of person, you then need to set some performance standards by which you can judge whether or not you are becoming that kind of person!

In a class I taught, for instance, a woman named Lorna said she wanted to become a friendlier person—a "be" goal. I questioned her further as to how she would recognize that she was friendlier. It soon became clear that in her mind this would include improving her ability to remember people's names. She had a hard time recalling names, so she tended to shy away from people—not wanting to reveal that she couldn't call them by anything more than "Hey, you." So we discussed methods to fix people's names in memory, such as writing the name down, using it several times in conversation, asking for the name more openly, or asking for people to spell their name.

Out of that "be" goal came some specific techniques by which Lorna could exercise friendliness. She set a goal of learning five persons' names per week as a deliberate exercise. At last report, she was pleased with her progress, because she knew exactly how to go about becoming a friendlier person in terms that were meaningful to her. As she took control of the situation, she found that other people were more responsive to her in turn and initiated conversations with her. Her "be" goal of becoming friendlier was becoming a reality.

"DO" GOALS

In addition to having "be" goals, most of us have certain things we want to accomplish. These can be either activities (learning how to play tennis or bridge) or tasks (set up a preschool program, read *War and Peace,* take a needlepoint class). One person might want to raise his income by 20 percent; another might desire to learn Russian; still another might yearn to see Paris in the springtime.

An amusing thing happened to me in a class I was teaching. It was the first time I had offered a class on "Managing Your Life," and about two hundred people had signed up for the two sections of the class. Those attending represented quite an age span, from teenagers to senior citizens.

A nice couple named John and Fran Williamson came to the first two sessions, and then I didn't notice them anymore. I didn't think too much about it, because a certain amount of attrition is to be expected in such a large class. A few weeks later, however, I received a note from Fran in which she explained their absence.

It seemed John and Fran had attended the first meeting and heard what I was saying about setting specific goals and working to fulfill those goals. And this couple had taken me seriously. They had taken a hard look at the fact that they had always wanted to travel but had never done so. Once they started thinking in that direction, they had become enthused about visiting Europe. Deciding time was precious, they had dropped out of my class and flown off to Europe—they just couldn't wait.

Fran's note to me indicated they would be happy to finish the course next time it was offered. She hoped that they would get as much out of the latter part of the class as they did out of the first two sessions!

What do you want to accomplish? Do you want to follow the John Muir Trail through the High Sierras? Learn to dance the Funky Chicken? Develop a magic act? Do mission work in Zaire? Write an exposé of arbitrage on Wall Street?

Write all your bright ideas down. Sort them out and live with them awhile. Try them on for size. Pray about them. Think about them. Get familiar with them. Write some of them on Post-It® notes and stick them on your phone, the dashboard of your car, or the refrigerator. In the next chapter we will describe how to process this laundry list of "do" goals into a useful list of priorities and a plan of attack.

═══ POSITIVE GOALS ═══

Goals should normally be stated positively, not negatively. This develops the proper mental attitude with which you approach the goal.

Say that George wants to lose ten pounds and is developing a diet he is going to follow. He should write his diet goals in the positive terms of what he is going to eat and what that will do for him, rather than in negative terms of what he is *not* going to do. Negative goals can be depressing, because they constantly remind you of the bad things in your life—the things you are trying to get away from. And when you feel depressed, it will be harder for you to take positive steps toward achieving your goals!

George should say, "My goal today is to eat three scrumptious meals that will total a thousand delicious calories. I will have a cup of decaffeinated coffee and a fruit medley and toast for breakfast. I will have a light salad and whole wheat bread for lunch. I will have four-to-six ounces of pasta and eight ounces of broccoli, beans, and cauliflower for dinner. Before I go to bed I will have a crisp apple. I commit myself to this plan because this will help me move toward my weight goal."

This is a positive affirmation; it states what is going to be done and why. Contrast it with another person's negative diet goal: "Today I am not going to eat any banana splits or peanut butter sandwiches or chocolate malts. No buttered Danish rolls for me —or any fantastic, gooey goodies . . . and on and on." All such a negative list would do is serve as a reminder of the things the dieter shouldn't be thinking about at all—as well as a reminder of the deprivation he or she is going through.

═══ AUTHENTIC GOALS ═══

When you set goals, it's easy to get snookered into listing goals you think you *should* have instead of goals that are truly authentic for you. You can list all kinds of way-out goals that sound elegant or noble but don't really reflect the kind of person you are and how you have been designed. Don't waste your time on such goals— they are not authentic!

I discovered the importance of authentic goals in my own life when it came to my preaching style. For the first six years of my preaching ministry, I worked many hours each week on polishing the manuscript text of my sermons. I would pray and study and then type out my sermon, go down to the church and rehearse it, polish it and retype it, so that the result would be a shimmering sermon that was grammatical, balanced, well worded, and stylistically impressive. On Sunday morning I would try to deliver it with a minimum of attention to the typescript, but adhering as much as possible to the finely honed lines I had written. I poured a lot of blood, sweat, and tears into the *way* I said things as well as into the content of what I said. My goal was to be a "polished preacher."

Then I had an opportunity to go to a ministers' convocation where there were two speakers. One was a celebrated pastor and writer who gave an outstanding polished sermon—a perfect example of what I had been trying to do. Here was that style elevated to the apogee of splendor. Frankly, I was impressed.

Then the second speaker arose to address us. A somewhat rumpled, red-headed Irish Quaker lawyer from Philadelphia, he carried to the platform a pile (more like an armload) of paper— clippings, notes, legal pads covered with notes, and that morning's *New York Times*. He opened up the *Times*, read a few paragraphs from the paper and commented on them. Next, he set the newspaper aside and rifled unceremoniously through his pile, hunting for some obscure clipping, on which he then commented.

This man's speech had no formal polish whatsoever. At first glance it even seemed to lack unity, coherence, and emphasis. He paused a number of times to hunt for items in his sliding stack of clippings. And yet this man's sermon communicated powerfully. He had a directness, an immediacy, an uninhibited personality, a unique potency that came crashing through to the listeners and made all of his lack of polish totally irrelevant. And this "unpolished" speaker kept our attention glued on him for one solid hour!

The Philadelphia lawyer's presentation was powerful because it was authentic communication. It came through, heart to heart, unstifled by formal concerns for preset phrasing, polish, or organizational niceties. Whereas the previous sermon had *impressed* me, this man's presentation *moved* me deeply.

From that day forth, my whole preaching style changed; I no longer preached from a polished, typed manuscript nor practiced the verbal delivery of a sermon. For in this man I had seen something of my authentic self. I realized I was frustrated in my preaching because my goals of polished delivery were not authentic for me. So from that point on I worried less about style and delivery and I concentrated more on content and direct, logical communication. For the first time I began to truly enjoy myself in the pulpit. My preaching became alive and dynamic for me and, I believe, more so for those who were listening.

Not that my style became exactly like the lawyer's—that's not the point. But in him I saw a man who was being true to his authentic communicating uniqueness. And it worked for him; in fact, it made the previous polished performance pale by contrast.

Through this experience, I reassessed my own gifts. I am a fairly verbal person who can think on my feet. I can plan ahead while I'm talking. I can speak passable (though not lyrical) prose and can usually avoid talking myself into truly terrible grammatical corners. God had given me spontaneous verbalizing abilities that I was not using. So I began to restructure my preaching goals. Consequently, my preparation time became more enriching, for in it I was saturating myself in the content and the logic and the dynamics of the message I felt God wanted me to deliver, rather than endlessly polishing the details of the delivery.

There are a couple of reasons we tend to get trapped into unauthentic goals: (1) We don't understand the gifts God has given us, or (2) We don't use them boldly. This is why the clarification process I spoke of in the previous chapter is so important. Among other things, we need to clarify that our goals are authentic and true to our God-given uniqueness.

LONG-RANGE AND INTERMEDIATE-RANGE GOALS

Where do you want to be five years from now? Ten years from now? Thirty years from now? Your long-range goals will help you keep on track toward that seemingly distant future.

One helpful way to focus on long-range goals is with the following exercise: Fantasize that you are a spry and vital 107 years old. You've had a long and fruitful career, and you are now ready for the ultimate retirement plan. They are going to celebrate your life and accomplishments with a community event and, as a part of this gala affair, a local paper is going to feature an article about you that tells what kind of person you are and what you have accomplished in your 107 years. (They don't think you can make it to 110—the next nice, round number!)

Now, as an exercise, write that article yourself. What would you like to have written about you as you sail into the shimmering sunset of your career? What kind of life would you like to be able to look back on at age 107? The article you write need not be long but it should cover the kind of person you want to have become ("be" goals) as well as the things you would like to have accomplished ("do" goals).

Out of this short article can then come a list of your life goals. Write them down in specific and measurable terms—and don't forget to date them. Regularly reviewing (and, when necessary, revising) your life goals can be extremely helpful in keeping your life moving in the direction you want it to move.

Now think backwards in shorter increments of time (five years, fifteen years, twenty-five years, and so forth) and identify some of the steps which could bring you to the accomplishment of those long-range goals. These would be your intermediate and short-term goals. They should be realistic, but they should also represent the deepest longings of your heart—not goals you think you "ought" to have, but what you sincerely desire to have happen. Which of these intermediate goals could you begin to work on right away?

═══ HOW BIG SHOULD GOALS BE? ═══

The objection is often raised, "Well, isn't setting big goals sort of silly—setting yourself up for a disappointment? After all, few people really accomplish anything big in life! Aren't you just stirring up idle and empty dreams people never can reach?"

My answer is no—as long as the goals chosen are realistic and accomplishable as well as big. By "realistic" I mean that other people have accomplished the same or similar goals—and that these goals are a reflection of *your* talents, interests, gifts, and aspirations.

I think it is better to set one's sights a shade too high, and know the exhilaration of having attempted something bigger than oneself, than to set one's sights so low that life is no challenge. Robert Schuller says, "I would rather attempt something big and fail than attempt nothing and succeed!" I like that. Life is richer when we are involved in mind-stretching, challenging tasks that are worthy of big people rather than shuffling through life, settling for unchallenging goals that mean precious little when they are attained.

Your goals should be big enough to make you stretch. Big enough to challenge you to exercise more of your potential. Big enough to help you accomplish some things that are important in your own eyes. As the poet said, "A man's reach should exceed his grasp, or else what's a heaven for?"

Besides, people *do* succeed at big goals! Some years back, for instance, Mrs. Joseph Birzler of Huntington Beach, California, began sewing clothing for children in World Vision's Korean orphanage. She set a big goal for herself—to have finished ten thousand dresses by the time she and her husband celebrated their fiftieth wedding anniversary on 1 August 1975. But by June 1974, "Aunt Rose" had already exceeded her goal by two hundred dresses!

The Birzlers established a clothing assembly line in their garage, and several volunteers helped Aunt Rose and her husband with their task. Together they made an average of two hundred twenty dresses every two months—about twenty-seven per day. Most of the material used was donated, and Aunt Rose emphasizes that not one inch of trim was wasted.

She and other volunteers also made over four thousand quilts for Korean orphans, and she broadened her ministry and began sending infant clothing to Vietnam. In spite of serious back trouble and failing eyesight, Aunt Rose was giving all she had for some of "the least ones" as a part of her promise to serve God as long as she was able.*

If you don't want to stretch, there's no point in setting goals. You can coast, float, and lie dead in the water without goals! The purpose of a goal is to help you move smartly toward a target you haven't reached yet.

So set goals that are realistic but challenging. Set goals that take some doing, but are achievable in bite-sized chunks. As Robert Schuller says, "Inch by inch, anything's a cinch!"

═══ WHERE DO WE GET OUR GOALS? ═══

PARENTS HELP US SET GOALS

For some, goals come from parents—from what they teach us about life and from the aspirations they have for us.

*"A Story of Ten Thousand Dresses," *World Vision Magazine*, June 1974, pp. 20, 21.

For instance, there are the parents who grew up the hard way —who were so impressed with the way they limited their own lives that they want to make sure their kids didn't make the same mistakes.

How often we have heard the complaint of the unschooled middle-aged immigrant parent, "I want my children to have it better than I did." They say to their kids, "Go to school. Get an education. Don't make the same mistakes I made."

This is a frequent theme in Studs Terkel's fascinating oral history, *Working*. Interview after interview with working people features deep-seated, passionate aspirations parents have for their children. For instance, Mike Lefevre, the steel worker, says:

> A mule, an old mule, that's the way I feel. . . . You know what I heard from more than one guy at work? "If my kid wants to work in a factory, I am going to kick the hell out of him." I want my kid to be an effete snob. . . . I want him to be able to quote Walt Whitman, to be proud of it.
>
> If you can't improve yourself, you improve your posterity. Otherwise life isn't worth nothing. You might as well go back to the cave and stay there. I'm sure the first caveman who went over the hill to see what was on the other side—I don't think he went there wholly out of curiosity. He went there because he wanted to get his son out of the cave. Just the same way I want to send my kid to college. . . .
>
> This is gonna sound square, but my kid is my imprint. . . . This is why I work. Every time I see a young guy walk by with a shirt and tie and dressed up real sharp, I'm looking at my kid, you know? That's it.*

Parents have the opportunity as well as the inclination to influence their children's goals in life. A young person's goals can be influenced by the example of a parent's life—as in the case of a child who wants to "follow in dad's (or mom's) footsteps" in a chosen field of endeavor or who determines to accomplish an objective a parent could never achieve. And parents can influence their children's goals by deliberate effort as well. In their effort to give their children opportunities they missed or help their children avoid mistakes they made, they can promote certain studies or relationships or patterns of behavior that become incorporated into their child's goals.

*Studs Terkel, *Working* (New York: Random House, 1972), pp. xxxvii–xxxviii.

A dramatic example of this can be found among the many refugees from Southeast Asia who have settled in the United States in recent years. These families, who have paid dearly for the opportunity of living in our country, have for the most part been very effective in teaching their children to value the opportunities of schooling here in their adopted country. As a result, it is common to read of outstanding academic achievement among the children of Southeast Asian refugees.

LIFE EXPERIENCES INFLUENCE OUR GOALS

Experiences can help us refine and/or radically change our goals.

For example, hardship or poverty in childhood can be a tremendous motivator and shaper of goals to get out of the ghetto or simply not to be poor. Playwright Moss Hart, the articulate late riser I quoted in an earlier chapter, was raised in grinding poverty in the Bronx. The boredom, drudgery, and indignities he observed at an early age instilled in him a deep desire not to be poor and helped him pursue his goal of escaping the squalid conditions of his childhood.

Hart writes of his first escape from the Bronx, at about age sixteen, to spend three months at Camp Utopia. The thought of leaving his dismal apartment for the green of the country so exhilarated him that he felt he had the strength of ten men:

> I realized suddenly and acutely that the summers had always been the worst time of all for me: the season of the year that I hated the most. There is anonymity about poverty in the wintertime; it remains hidden behind drawn curtains or blinds. But in the summer the choking heat of the tenements sends it sprawling out onto the stoops and fire escapes and sidewalks, to be nakedly exposed for the offense and the ugliness that it is. I knew now why I had always dreaded the approach of warm weather, but as this particular spring deepened into early summer, I could almost sniff the aroma of country meadows even in the bowels of the subway or in my cubbyhole at the *New York Times*.
>
> When the great day arrived at last for us to leave for Camp Utopia, the moisture in my eyes which my mother mistook for filial sentiment (it was to be my first long absence away from the family) was, I suppose, actually something akin to tears of joy at getting . . . out.
>
> Rarely have I set forth on a journey with such a lift of the heart. Innocence, however, always carries the seeds of its own destruction and I carried mine to Camp Utopia that glistening summer's day, like Dick Whittington approaching London with his heart on

his sleeve and his possessions on his back, hearing nothing but the
lovely sound of Bow bells in the distance.*

Like Moss Hart, I found that some of my early experiences
were formative in the shaping of my personal goals. In particular, working at many different jobs in my early years helped give
me a sense of what I eventually wanted out of life. I began by
mowing lawns and delivering papers, then worked in a grocery
store and a butcher shop. Later I served as a florist, a cab driver,
a parking attendant, a grease monkey. I was a minimum wage
laborer in a frozen food factory, a bank janitor and night watch-
man, and a library page. I worked outdoors as a carpenter's
helper in the hot, smoggy summer's heat of Southern California
and as a ditch digger in the cold, windy rains of Seattle—as well
as indoors in retail stores, offices, and churches.

I don't regret any of these jobs. From them, I learned things I
would never have learned otherwise. I met people. And out of
those twenty-plus jobs I held from childhood through my mid-
twenties, I discovered a great deal about what I wanted to do
with my life and the kinds of things I wanted to accomplish—not
to mention the kinds of things *I wanted nothing more to do with!*
So in a sense, they all helped motivate me and shape my goals.

It is also possible—indeed, to be expected—that our experiences may change our goals. Goals, as we pursue them, can come
to seem of less value than we once thought. (For example, a man
can set out after an abundance of material possessions and then
discover that they don't bring the kind of satisfaction he expected.) Or new goals may emerge that take higher priority than
the old ones.

By age forty-eight, John Z. DeLorean had worked his way up
the corporate ladder at General Motors to become a vice president with a salary of $550,000 per year. But in the process of
coming into that plush corporate environment high in the ivory
tower, he found his goals changing. Just being at the top and
making a lot of money were not what he wanted most anymore,
so he decided to make a change. He quit his job and took a
position as the unsalaried head of a voluntary group involved in
persuading corporations to hire disabled people. And then, as
many people know from following the headlines, he changed
direction several more times—his troubles have been writ large

*Moss Hart, *Act One* (New York: Random House, 1959), pp. 134–135.

in the pages of the tabloids. I find his story fascinating as the tale of a man in search of a better set of goals. There are several books that tell DeLorean's story, including Patrick Wright's *On a Clear Day You Can See General Motors* and DeLorean's own book, *DeLorean.**

Jack Fuller is still another example of how goals can change through experience. Jack had a comfortable life selling caps and gowns in Ohio. Then, at age forty, he changed his goals. He and his family moved to Alaska, where he took up life on the frozen Bering Sea. Now he says they may move to the Virgin Islands someday.[†]

I have seen a similar process of goal changing at work among my colleagues in the ministry over the years. An associate pastor in a large church will put in ten to fifteen years working toward the goal of becoming a senior preaching pastor. Then, when that goal is accomplished, the same pastor will find that the pressures of weekly preaching and heavy administrative duties force him to reassess his goals and go back to being an associate. I have also seen the opposite happen—preachers from small churches who flee into staff roles at larger churches to heal from unhappy experiences with their congregations, only to realize they will never be content until they are preaching every week.

GOD'S WORD

Meditation on the Bible has formed and transformed the goals of many. As we commit ourselves to Jesus Christ, his values increasingly become a source for determining the direction of our lives— and therefore our goals. And our primary source for those values is God's Word. As we read the Word, we are motivated to direct our lives along the paths that are pleasing to God:

> Therefore I tell you, do not be anxious about your life, what you shall eat or what you shall drink, nor about your body, what you shall put on. Is not life more than food, and the body more than clothing? (Matt. 6:25).

> Go therefore and make disciples of all nations, baptizing them in the name of the Father and of the Son and of the Holy Spirit,

*Patrick Wright, *On a Clear Day You Can See General Motors* (New York: Avon, 1980); John Z. DeLorean, *DeLorean* (Grand Rapids, MI: Zondervan, 1985).
[†]Wilbur Bradbury, *The Adult Years* (New York: Time-Life Books, 1975), p. 117.

teaching them to observe all that I have commanded you; and lo, I am with you always, to the close of the age (Matt. 28:19–20).

Set your minds on things that are above, not on things that are on earth. . . . put on love, which binds everything together in perfect harmony. . . . And whatever you do, in word or deed, do everything in the name of the Lord Jesus, giving thanks to God the Father through him (Col. 3:2, 14, 17).

ULTIMATELY, YOUR GOALS DEPEND ON YOU

In the final analysis, our goals are decided by us alone. While we may be strongly influenced by our parents and by our own experiences, in the end our goals proceed from the bottom-line choices we make.

We should not look at goal selection as a passive process in which we are helpless victims, but as one of the truly great opportunities of life. When we set goals, we are taking the responsibility to decide what we will do with our lives. As God challenged the people of Israel in Deuteronomy, "I have set before you life and death, blessing and curse; therefore choose life, that you and your descendants may live" (Deut. 30:19).

═══ CHOOSING AND PRIORITIZING GOALS ═══

The ability to make choices and decisions is important and valuable. It is a high compliment from God that he gave us this power, and we need to choose responsibly in light of the faith he places in us.

I cannot tell you what your specific goals should be. Hopefully, the following exercise on prioritizing goals will assist you somewhat in understanding the process of making good goal choices. It can help clarify the process so that your choosing is not done unconsciously, but thoughtfully, with care and understanding of your personal alternatives.

One of the most important aspects of choosing goals is to understand the process of clarifying and sorting out the various elements of your life as discussed in chapter 6. The processes of clarification and goal setting support each other.

Here is an exercise that will help you sort out some of your goals and rank them according to priority. Start with the short list of goals (short-term, intermediate, and long-range) you wrote at the beginning of this chapter, and expand your list to include a total of fifteen or twenty goals that appeal to you. Your "brainstorming" list can also be helpful at this point, and you can also include the goals that emerged when you wrote the article about your retirement at age 107.

Once you have expanded your list, you should have a hopper full of goals. There are probably some which are long-range, some shorter range. Some may be trivial, others profound. Some are easily "doable," others much more formidable.

The next step is to sort out this miscellaneous list of goals so that you can focus on the more important ones and begin to make some progress in working toward them.

As I mentioned in the previous chapter, one of the critical problems in our age is the proliferation of opportunities. Many people think they can be twentieth-century Renaissance persons—latter-day Leonardo da Vincis; they think they can "have it all." They fail to make some hard decisions among a lot of good options and, as a result, they dissipate their time and energy—and set themselves up to fail.

Good as it is to have a clear list of twenty goals—if you try to achieve *all* of them in a short time, you will probably drop in your tracks. If you want to learn to speak Chinese, become a vocational guidance counselor, open up a chain of aluminum siding outlets—and accomplish all these goals by next spring—you are almost certainly doomed to failure.

The simple fact is that no one can "do it all"—at least, not at once! Every one of your goals may be stunning and worthwhile, but to make any progress you must prioritize them according to two considerations—importance and feasibility. The goals you should start with are those which are strongest in both considerations—they are both important and feasible.

Once you start the prioritizing process, you will probably find that some items on your list will have to wait because they are extremely low on one or the other of these scales. One item might go to the bottom of the priority list because, though it is important to you, it is one of the least feasible (like buying a customized Boeing 747). Another item might be passed on for now because, though it is feasible, it is not as valuable to you.

Chart A is designed to help you sort out your goal list. First, write a shortened form of each goal by name in the first column (under "Name of Goal").

Next, evaluate the importance of each goal according to the scale below (it's OK to assign the same number to more than one goal) and write the number in the column marked "I" on the chart:

Chart A
PRIORITIZING GOALS

Name of Goal	I 5–10	F 0–10	F + I Score	Final Ranking

IMPORTANCE SCALE

10 A MUST. This is really crucial—"The Biggy."
 9 I could live without it, but it would be difficult.
 8 This is important.
 7 This is worth some hard work—more than a six.
 6 This is worth *some* effort to make happen.
 5 I would like it, but I won't die if I don't get it.

The reason the importance scale is ranked from just 5 to 10 (rather than 1 to 10) is that we are assuming anything that got onto this list would be worth at least a five to you!

(Another way to discriminate this importance factor is to compare the goal with any long-range goals you have formulated. Generally people's long-range goals represent their wisest and most deeply considered goals.)

Now, evaluate the *feasibility* of each goal. What do we mean by feasibility? A goal is feasible if, all things considered (your age, your gifts, your place in life, and so forth), it is *realistic* to think it *could* be done. Some items on your list will be more feasible for you than others.

Interpret the feasibility of each goal using the scale below and write the result in the column marked "F." Unlike the importance scale, the feasibility scale goes from 0 to 10. This is because some goals, though very important to you, may not be feasible at all—at least not at this point in your life.

FEASIBILITY SCALE

10   This is really a possibility. It would take little effort. I could do it with one eye closed and one hand tied to my side.

9   I could do it, but I would have to work a bit at it.

8   It could be done—but I would get sweaty.

7   This would require concerted time, energy, sweat, and perseverance.

6   This one is harder than 7, but the odds are better than even that I could do it.

5   Even odds as to whether I could do it. A 50 percent chance of completing this.

4   This would require a pyrotechnic sawdust-trail conversion to motivate me, but if that happened it could be done.

3   Not too feasible. Would require *minor miracle* (parting of bath water).

2   Not very feasible. Would require *major miracle* (parting of small lake).

1   Not really feasible at all. Would require *gigantic miracle* (parting of Red Sea, confirmed by numerous Arab witnesses).

0   About as much chance as growing hair on a billiard ball or discovering a cure for cancer in my garage—virtually impossible.

When you have come up with an importance number and a feasibility number for each goal, *add the two numbers together* and enter the sum in the column marked "I + F." Then, in the last column, list the goals in order of the I + F score, starting with the highest number.

The purpose of this exercise is to *flag* for you those two or three goals that combine both *high importance* and *high feasibility*. (They will be at the top of your list in the right-hand column on the chart.) These are undoubtedly the goals you should begin with.

Why? Because if you begin to work on a goal that is important but very difficult, you may soon give up and get discouraged. If you begin by working on something that is feasible but less important, the motivating challenge will be hard to sustain. It is therefore imperative that your first foray into the process of intentionally enriching your life through systematically pursuing goals have as much going for it as possible.

You will have, as a result of this exercise, a "process priority list"—a list of goals in priority order, beginning with the highest priority. (This is the list you ended up with in the right-hand column of chart A.) I suggest that you process these goals into your life only one at a time, starting at the top of the list. In the chapters to come we will look at the positive steps we can take toward making our goals a reality.

═══ SUMMARY ═══

Papillon stood on the cliff with his friends. His long-term goal was escape and freedom. His short-term goal was to grab his raft of coconuts and catch Lisette, the super wave to freedom.

A goal is a future state or event that you seek to accomplish. It can be measured in time and by performance standards. Goals should be clear, not fuzzy. They should be written in pencil, reviewed regularly and modified. They should be positive, authentic, and designed for a specific time period (short-term, intermediate, or long-range). They should be big enough to allow you to stretch without being unrealistic.

We are influenced in our choice of goals by our parents and our past experiences—but in the end we must accept responsibility for the goals we choose today and tomorrow. In order to live confidently in a hostile world, you need to be clear as to what goals you could pursue to enrich *your* life.

Processing *8* into a Plan

By now you have not only a set of goals, but a "process priority list" which tells you where you should begin. A confident and affable attitude toward life doesn't just happen; it is planned. Papillon didn't just toss his bundle of coconuts into the surf on the spur of the moment; catching Lisette at the right moment took careful planning.

This brings you to the vital step of processing the first of your goals. Out of this process will emerge further clarification and a plan of attack.

Let me guess something about the goal you have settled on as number one. If you are like many people I have had in my classes, the goal you've selected is no stranger to you. It probably represents an old familiar dream that somehow you just haven't gotten around to doing anything about. But this time you have determined to have a real go at it. Terrific! There is a process available that will help you make a potent plan that can work to make that dream a reality!

=== STARTING THE PLAN ===

First, break the goal down into a series of *logical steps* —steps that make sense to you—and pin some specific dates to those steps.

Say your goal is to visit Europe. You need to set an appropriate date and then some intermediate dates for gathering data, choosing an itinerary, and building a realistic savings plan.

Or perhaps your goal is to open your own gas station and minimarket on Interstate 5 near Buttonwillow, California. You will need to break down the task into such appropriate steps as these:

114

(1) Define the goal

(2) Gather information (library, articles, interviews, small business courses, etc.)

(3) List the alternative approaches

(4) Rank the alternatives

(5) Choose the best alternative

(6) Locate a corner, a company, a franchise

(7) Gain training and/or experience (i.e., get a job in a service station, take a continuing education class in small business management)

(8) Develop a financing plan

(9) Raise the capital

List your steps in logical or calendar order. Now, turn to one of the first steps and ask yourself the question, "If it were impossible to fail at this task—what would I begin to do to accomplish this step?" Then write down the steps you would take to accomplish this first step.

As you try to do this, you might find yourself saying, "Wait a minute; I'm not sure I know what all the right steps are." If you don't, then the next thing you need to do is *find an expert* in the field—whether in person or through a book—who can answer these questions for you.

If you don't know where to find an expert, start asking your friends—they might know where an expert can be located. Ask a librarian for help. Look in the catalog of a local college or business school for courses or information centers that might help you. Or even try the yellow pages! You will find that knowledgeable help *is* available all around you. *Ask for help.* People are willing to give it.

I'll never forget the story of Steve Prine who, in the middle of the oil shortage in the early 1970s, decided to become an oil broker. He was only in his early twenties, and all he had to start with was a phone and a garage apartment. So he started by calling presidents of small and medium-sized oil companies, asking them if they had any oil to sell or if they wanted to buy any—and how much. Then he told them he was a young man just starting out, and he needed some advice; he asked them how to become an oil broker. After calling about a hundred oil company executives, he had a list of those who wanted oil, those who had oil to sell, and some high-quality personal tutoring on how to put a deal together. In a few months he had made more than a million dollars! He went to the top and asked for help—and he got it.

Breaking down your goal into specific parts and gathering information are the first steps in laying down a plan for reaching your goal. All but the very simplest goals are best achieved with a written, 1-2-3 plan. An excellent detailed (though dated) manual on planning is *Let's Rap on Planning*, published by the General Council of the Presbyterian Church, U. S. It focuses specifically on church planning, but the general principles would apply to any kind of planning.*

Let's Rap on Planning points out that planning involves several of the steps described above: Define the goal(s); List alternative ways to achieve the goal(s) Choose the best alternative; Formulate the action plan; Implement and monitor the action plan.

Remember, good planning is not an accident. It may seem awkward at first, so allow yourselves room for mistakes and setbacks. You will find that in the long run the time you spend planning pays big dividends.

FLAG THE VULNERABLE SPOTS

After you have gathered the steps of your plan and written them down, look over the steps and ask yourself, "If this plan were to be royally and routinely screwed up by me—where would I most likely mess it up?" Or, to put it another way—"If there is a weak spot in the plan, a place where I would tend to get off the track—where would that dangerous spot be located?"

And right there—at that spot—plant a warning flag, or circle the step in red. Then, having located the thin ice in your scheme, spell out for yourself a corrective program designed to *get you past that vulnerable spot*.

This is a crucial technique, because countless people have found that in their attempts to reach their high-priority goals, they have invariably *fallen by the wayside* at the *same spot* time and time again. They continued to get derailed at that spot because they did not plan ahead of time to take extra precautions when they reached their "rough spot."

*341 Ponce De Leon Avenue, N.E., Atlanta, GA 30308. Or get hold of Alan Lakein's *How to Get Control of Your Time and Your Life* and read chapter 4, "Control Starts with Planning." Another source of help in the area of planning is Gary Emory, *Own Your Own Life* (New York: New American Library, 1982), especially chapter 3, "Step Two: Choice."

The point is that a plan must be realistic to deal with your unique needs and patterns—and especially to deal with your unique weaknesses. And these are dealt with best by knowing precisely where the potential traps are located, labeling them, and being prepared with a procedure to counter the problem.

Larry Sheldon sells life insurance, and for a number of years had been a rather mediocre salesman. He knew what he should be doing, but he often got into a familiar rut. His plan for selling involved such steps as gathering a prospect list, making initial contacts with those on the prospect list, weeding out the unlikely prospects, and then systematically nurturing the most likely candidates. But Larry's problem was that instead of diligently following up on the really good prospects he had labeled, he found himself devoting too much time to tending his "glass eggs." (A glass egg is a prospective customer who is easy to deal with—friendly, kind, affirming, easy to get in to see—but who you know, in the long run, is never going to "hatch"—or buy a policy.)

Larry would take a few initial swipes at the authentic (and therefore challenging) prospects, but he wouldn't persevere to see if they were for real. It was almost as if he were afraid to really push to close the deal because if they said "No" and he lost them as prospects, he knew he wouldn't really have any good prospects left. So he stalled and unconsciously avoided attempting to close a deal with them. He kept telling himself they needed a bit more time to ripen, a bit more loving care . . . and then he would turn to give a loving stroke of service to an old familiar "glass egg" in the proven false hope of getting business there.

Larry's new plan involved flagging his glass-egg tendency and persevering through his real prospect list at the rate he knew he should be going. He soon discovered that he did, as a matter of fact, go through his prospect list much faster, which meant he had to do more prospecting—but it also meant a rise in sales and pay when he did it.

USE STRUCTURES

One way you can plan your life more efficiently is to set up and use *structures*. By structures I mean *habitual patterns* or methods planned ahead of time and carried out regularly. Structures are like miniature, built-in, repeatable plans—in computer terms, they are like "macros." When you have a structure, you don't have to re-invent the wheel daily; you can carry out certain functions without having to pay specific attention to them.

Everyone's life is different and will require its own structures. But if they are there, and they are well thought out, they will save you countless hours and a great deal of anxiety.

I saw an illustration of this principle a number of years ago when I was visiting my brother in Colorado. While there, we visited a friend of his named George, who had a business of mounting large, exotic South American butterflies in Lucite display boxes. To put together one of the sets involved precise cutting, heating, gluing, and assembling—and the finished product looked beautiful. As I watched George at work, I saw that the process was simplified by a series of precut assembly tools that held and guided the boxes so handily that a young boy could put them together—as a matter of fact, *was* doing so.

The key was that the assembly process had been set up carefully in advance by means of a set of guard rails, assembly boxes, jigs, and so on, that helped make it all happen neatly, easily, and precisely. Here was a plan that was built into a set of physical structures that guided the assembly process and made the complex job almost easy.

TASK STRUCTURES

I have found several kinds of structures useful in my own life and work. One structure is to routinely carry out certain tasks in certain places.

For instance, I have an office and a study. My office is at the church and my study is at home. And I have found that I work more happily, efficiently, and productively if I do certain kinds of things in my office and others in my study.

At the office, I feel a need to spend time with my door open, available to my colleagues. One of the main things I do at the office is get interrupted. Now, that would be very frustrating to me if I needed not to be interrupted. But when I go to the office I generally plan on doing those kinds of things that allow for interruptions. I save the kinds of work that need to be carried out without interruption—my heavy reading, thinking, studying, praying, and decision making—to be done at home in my study.

PAPER STRUCTURES

Another structure has to do with the handling of paper. I get lots of mail, notes, memos, magazines, books. In fact, I sometimes believe that papers have procreative powers and that they breed overnight when I'm not looking.

In my very messy-desk phase of life (which I've been in and out of most of the time over the past thirty years) my chaotic system involves my handling many papers over and over again. When I'm functioning best, however, I use some structures that cut down on the repetitive paper shuffling.

The process starts with the coming of the mail. I look through the mail while standing over a trash basket, and probably one half to two thirds of the mail drops immediately into the "round file." A great deal of time can be salvaged by not even opening some mail! If I pick up notes at the inter-office mail slot, I try to glance over them and answer them right then and there without carrying them back to my desk (where they're liable to get lost). When I have dealt with the mail that can be discarded or answered immediately, I then put the papers that are left in the appropriate place for dealing with them.

Which brings us to my second structure for handling paper . . . One day my friend Tom Horton was meeting with me in my office—on a day when my desk was particularly piled high with papers. He looked at my paper mountain and observed, "Jim, every paper on that desk represents an *unmade* decision." I thought about that and came to recognize at least the partial truth of Jim's statement.

Those heaped-up papers also represented the world's most *unorganized reminder system*. I had developed an unhealthy pattern where I couldn't put anything away because I was counting on the papers being out and visible to remind me of something I had to do.

If there was a contract to review, for instance, I would leave the contract out in plain sight so I wouldn't forget to read it. My way of using this unorganized reminder system was to periodically shuffle through the papers and see if there was a crisis I was in danger of missing or an issue ripened to near-disaster status. Then I would deal with the problem and put the rest of the papers back in the stack to sift through again at a later date.

This system (one of the *tried and false* systems common to the American way of life) had some obvious weaknesses. It was unreliable, disorganized, and left me in a state of anxiety that important matters might get misplaced.

The structure that I evolved to counter the heaped-up-paper syndrome was the habit of weeding out the incoming papers and tasks as soon as possible. The rule of thumb is to handle each paper *only once* if at all possible—and to be continually on guard against allowing too many exceptions to this rule. Instead of shuffling papers again and again, the idea is to make a decision about each one and dispose of it.

I have to admit that I still fall out of this system—regularly—and revert to my old paper shuffling. But I have learned that the way I handle the paper on my desk is a barometer of how much I am in or out of control of my life in general. When I am functioning well, I am functioning within the structure of handling paper immediately. When I am snowed, it is often because I have neglected the structure and let the papers pile up.

PLANNING STRUCTURES

Once the old paper-shuffling reminder routine is eliminated, how do I keep track of all the things I need to do and make sure they get done?

To come up with a workable daily system, I had to make a few brilliant discoveries for myself, sort of like re-inventing the wheel. One of the discoveries was a *pencil*, another was a *sheet of paper*, the third was a *system* by which I could employ these two in an orderly manner. A fourth was that most esoteric of entities—the *file folder*. Amazing, isn't it?

In order for my system to work, certain things needed to happen. First, I had to convince myself that a file folder was the best storage implement for a piece of paper that needed to be saved. Second, I had to convince myself that the decisions I faced and the actions I had to take in my work could be catalogued into a meaningful order. (That has been very hard for me; I tend to be very ambivalent about how to file things.)

I had to recognize that there were not that many ways to approach any and all items that came across my desk. In my work they boiled down to seven. Virtually every operation I was involved in could fit under one of the following categories:

- Telephone someone;
- Study and/or write something (memo, letter, report, sermon);
- Perform an errand inside the office—something in which my body had to get up from the desk and move about on the work premises (such as look at the broken slide on the playground);
- Perform an errand off-premises (visit the hospital, pick up the laundry, drop by the bookstore);

SAMPLE PLANNING SHEET

DO IT   Date _____

PHONE

_____

_____

_____

_____

_____

_____

WRITE

_____

_____

_____

_____

_____

DECIDE

_____

_____

_____

_____

_____

HOLD

_____

_____

_____

_____

_____

OFFICE ERRANDS

_____

_____

_____

_____

_____

OUTSIDE ERRANDS

_____

_____

_____

_____

_____

CONFER WITH

_____

_____

_____

_____

_____

VISIT

_____

_____

_____

_____

_____

- Confer (in house) with and/or delegate something to an assistant;
- Make a decision;
- Hold for future thought, decision, or action (put on back burner).

(Obviously you could regroup this list to suit your situation, combining or eliminating any of the categories, but this basic system works for me.)

I then proceeded to design a planning sheet that reflected the kinds of things I needed to do and organized these tasks into a meaningful structure.

Everything I need to do is noted on this planning sheet, and the papers that pertain to the task are filed away until they are needed. I keep my planning sheet right in front of me on my desk, and I keep it in a handy place to remind me what I have to do. Then, once or twice a week (sometimes more, if a lot is going on) I rewrite my planning sheet to reflect new tasks and new priorities.

REMINDER STRUCTURES

Another structure I have found helpful is to build into life a system to help me remember ideas, phone numbers, needs, and other miscellaneous bits of information that come to us throughout the day.

One structure of this type I have often used is a simple set of 3 × 5 cards which I try to keep in my breast pocket. When an idea comes to mind, or a need arises to call someone or write a memo—I jot it down on a card. (Women would probably find it simpler to carry a card pack or small notebook in their purse.) Then at regular intervals I will either file the card in the appropriate place or transfer the note onto my planning sheet.

There are many other areas in our lives where reminder structures as simple as a notebook, a date book, or similar tool can become a real asset. Many have even begun using their personal computers to keep track of notes and tasks for them—although, of course, this works best if you already spend a large portion of your time in touch with your computer.

Elton Trueblood, in his book *While It Is Day*, tells the story of an interview he had regarding an important decision of his career with President Faunce of Brown University:

One incident in my memorable interview with President Faunce has stayed in my mind, though I am sure it did not stay in his. While we were talking on the subject which was highly important for my career, I was shocked to see the great man suddenly stop speaking, take out a notebook, and write in it for three or four minutes, while I sat in silence. When he had finished writing, President Faunce again spoke to me, asking my pardon for his seeming discourtesy. Then he explained that ideas were his capital and that he had suddenly had an idea not connected with our immediate conversation. He went on to say that he had learned to put down ideas when they came because otherwise they might be lost forever. Far from being hurt, as he feared I might be, I was immensely grateful. With rare exceptions I have carried a *notebook* ever since and have learned that my ideas are not retained unless they are recorded.*

As one wag put it, "A short pencil is better than a long memory."

Reminders work best in our lives when we plan them so as to make them semi-automatic. Some of these are very simple little mechanical devices—as simple as a mileage notebook hanging on the cigarette lighter in the car. Each morning when you get in the car and reach down to turn on the ignition, you practically brush the hanging notebook with your hand. This built-in or structured positioning of the notebook reminds you to write down your mileage from the previous day's travel and to log the number of business miles for income tax records. If the notebook were buried in a desk in your office, you would have to remember to enter the mileage each day and would often forget it. But having it hang right over the ignition automatically reminds you of this brief daily chore.

One final warning, however. Whatever method you use—index cards, notebook, or computer—it is important to develop some orderly method of incorporating those messages into your life. This will probably mean transferring your notes on a regular basis onto your "To Do" list, your daily calendar, or whatever schedule structure you use.

A number of years ago, at my last church, I had a cartoon mounted on the wall. It showed a man in an office sitting behind a desk when someone has come in to tell him something. The man's entire desk is covered with little notes, lined row after

*Elton Trueblood, *While It Is Day* (New York: Harper & Row, 1974), p. 24.

row, literally hundreds of them covering the desk. He responds to the person who has entered his office by saying, "Let me make a note of that!"

Remember, the point of notes is not simply to make notes! The purpose of a reminder structure is to keep you from forgetting important information. Try to set it up so that it does its job!

TIME-USE STRUCTURES

Structures can also help us handle those repetitious events of life so we can use our time more efficiently.

I discovered long ago that I tend to work best when I give myself to a certain kind of work for significant blocks of time. Therefore, in planning my day, I ordinarily set aside chunks of time for certain activities. (That is one reason I divide my "To Do" list into groups of similar projects.) For example, I will plan a certain period of time for making telephone calls. Then I begin at the top of my phone list and start calling until I have attempted as many calls as I can.

I also write best in spurts. So I usually do any memo or letter writing early in the morning or late at night at home in preparation for the next day. I read and write sermons away from the office in my basement "hidey-hole" where my writing time is less likely to be interrupted. And for large writing projects I try to get away for an extended, uninterrupted period of time.

There are many other ways that time use can be structured. My friend Jim has a very active family with four children. As they were growing up, his kids were involved in the typical teenage and children's activities—Little League, soccer, school carnivals, and so on. In addition, the family was fully engaged in church activities. Along the way, they discovered that, depending on how they structure their time, the weekends could be either relaxing and regenerative or overactive, crammed, and exhausting.

So they developed some guidelines. One of the most important ones had to do with their discovery that if Jim and Carol went out on both Friday and Saturday nights the weekend usually turned out to be a bummer. So they decided they would go out on either Friday or Saturday, but not both. When they adopted this policy, they found they enjoyed the weekends more—with less chaos.

DECISION STRUCTURES

There is a significant principle involved in this whole matter of developing structures. In essence, structures are wise, well-thought-out decisions made in advance. If we do not have them—we tend to be constantly making decisions off the top of our heads and in the heat of the moment. This adds to our stress level and lessens the chances that our decisions would be good ones.

Early in our marriage my wife and I made some bad deals buying things (such as encyclopedias) from door-to-door salesmen. On a couple of other occasions we bought furniture on the spur of the moment and later were not too pleased with our decision. We realized that part of our displeasure in both instances came from the fact that we had bought impulsively and not wisely. So we made a rule for ourselves about any major purchases: Always sleep on it. Never make a large investment after only one showing. Go home, talk about it, think it over, get a good night's sleep. And then, if you are still agreed, go back and purchase it.

Of course, the salesman will always tell us that the sale ends in ten minutes, or that this is the last one available on the North American continent. Most of the time, we have found, that simply is not true. But even if we miss a bargain or two, we have found that in the long run we are more satisfied with a structured approach we've agreed on than with trying to make decisions with the pressure on.

PLACE STRUCTURES

There is a famous old saying—a place for everything, and everything in its place. That is not an idle, nit-picking saying. In our busy lives we lose the scissors, we move the scotch tape, we misplace a book. And later, when we need to lay our hands on the scissors or tape or book we can't remember where they are. Much time and effort can be saved if every object has a regular "home" where it is returned after use and can dependably be found.

I have always been fascinated by time and motion studies. My first interest in this came when I was a teenager. My father died when I was thirteen years old, my two older brothers had gone off to the war, and my mother had to go to work. This meant that I had to do the cooking, washing, house cleaning, ironing, and so on for my mother and my little sister.

Every Saturday I cleaned the house from stem to stern, and I got it down to a science. As all housewives know, a large portion of house cleaning involves putting things back in their place, and this is especially true when two of the three members of the family are children. I developed a procedure whereby I would never carry anything across the house to another room.

I usually started with the kitchen, and our kitchen had three doors. One went into the living room, one led to the dining room, and one opened toward the back of the house and the bedrooms. While cleaning the kitchen I would never leave that room. Anything that went toward the living room was piled at that door. Anything headed for the back rooms was piled at that door. And then I did not move anything until I went—*once*—to the room where it belonged. On that trip I took all the implements I needed for cleaning that room, as well as all the misplaced items that belonged there.

Being an essentially lazy teenager I worked at reducing my motions to the minimum. In fact, if the truth were known, trying to do as much as possible with as little wasted motion almost turned the whole cleaning project into a game—a sort of time and motion solitaire where each Saturday I worked against the clock to see how quickly I could clean the house and get the washing and ironing done. And this was in the days of stationary tubs, bluing rinse, pressure rollers on the washing machine, and hanging the clothes out on the line in the backyard if it wasn't raining and in the basement if it was raining (which in Seattle was a regular option)!

I'm sure you have some of the place patterns built into your life as well—a place where the incoming mail is always put, so that members of the family can go through it to see if there's a letter for them; a place where the suitcases are always stored, so that when you go on a trip you know where to look; a drawer in which your hankies can be found.

All of us have these patterns regarding place. The only problem is that some of us have a more chaotic or inconsistent system than others. Our lives run more effectively when these structures of place are clearly understood by all persons involved.

Some time back my buddy, Jim, and his wife, Carol, had their kitchen/family room rebuilt, and in the process they set up a new system of place structures. They live in a large two-story house that requires considerable walking just to get from one end to the other. The family room is one of the important centers where people (and things) tend to collect, but it is at the far end of the first floor, a long way from the bedrooms.

So Jim and Carol had built into the family room a set of six bins —one for each member of the family. Then if they found a sweater, a book, a school paper, or a second-hand all-day-sucker that belonged to a given member of the family—they just tossed it in that person's bin, and he or she could pick it up when it was missed. This system saved a lot of steps and a good deal of frustration— especially for Carol.

STRUCTURES FOR AVOIDING DISTRACTIONS

Another thing that can be dealt with by means of prior structuring is distractions. If you are anything like I am, you can be distracted by things lying about that need to be done. One of the structures I have built into my life when the pile gets too high on my desk is to put all the piled-up distractions in a box and temporarily stow them out of sight where they do not bother me while I can't attend to them. Then later that night (or mañana) I take out the box and sort through and deal with them (or, if possible, get my wife to sort them!).

There are myriad ways to structure your life to get rid of distractions. File the paper away if you are not working on it. If you don't want interruptions, shut the door. If you can't shut the door, go down to the public library and do your work. If your cronies hang out at the library, go to the library in the next town. The point is—if you really need privacy for what you are doing— *you* are responsible to make it happen.

I write best when I get my mind away from the press of the daily distractions of my work. So I am writing this chapter in a room of the Bahia Hotel in San Diego overlooking Mission Bay, where I have hidden myself away for a part of my study leave. I have only had about three phone calls all week and no mail. And so far I have written about twenty-two thousand words!

Still another way to deal with distractions is to enlist someone to protect you—your wife, your secretary, your brother or sister. In other words, if you can't fend off distractions by yourself—get help! Most of the time others will be happy to help you if you say you must concentrate on something without distraction.

Or try a sign on the door. One of my seminary professors had a sign that read, "I'm sure you have important things to do. I know I do. Why don't you go away and do them!" Admittedly, it was terse, but it was effective in cutting down interruptions.

An important thing to realize about structuring life to avoid distractions is that some environments can be inherently distracting. I had to face this issue myself when I was choosing a place to go on my study weekend. There were many options to choose from, and one would have been to stay at home to work. But at home there would be the normal intrusion of family and my all-too-close job. It would be too handy for people to get to me with everyday tasks. And I would be tempted to go over to the office and look at the mail each day.

Another possibility was to go to a cabin in the mountains or out in the desert. There would be a minimum of distractions, but also not much to do in the off hours besides go for a walk. Frankly, I didn't want that much aloneness.

So as a compromise I settled on San Diego. There I was away from home and work. Yet when I wanted a break there were some conveniences nearby—a theater, a beach to walk on, restaurants to sit in and read the paper and enjoy a cup of tea.

LEARNING TO BUILD IN STRUCTURES

Structures can be found in many kinds of things. They can be bulletin boards, whose function is to remind you now; calendars and date books, whose function is to remind you later; slot systems or pigeonholes, whose function is to let you get rid of things or pass them on efficiently to other people who are not immediately available. Structures can be *rules of thumb, principles* to which you have committed yourself, or *new habits* you have deliberately acquired.

Structures may seem like a bother at first. And it is true that setting up a structure involves a certain amount of time and thought. But once the structure becomes a natural part of your habit patterns, you won't have to think about it at all, and you will save large amounts of time and energy in the process. In the long run, structures can simplify your life by taking care of the details of your life for you and leaving you free to concentrate on your goals. So develop your own structures and make them your servants.

As a start in learning to build structures into your life, try this exercise. List ten areas of your life that could be simplified by imposing some structure. Then, for each, write one idea of how you could structure that area.

AREA NEEDING STRUCTURING	POSSIBLE SOLUTION
1. _____	_____
2. _____	_____
3. _____	_____
4. _____	_____
5. _____	_____
6. _____	_____
7. _____	_____
8. _____	_____
9. _____	_____
10. _____	_____

WHAT KINDS OF THINGS CAN BE STRUCTURED?

One of the first objections many people give to any kind of serious structuring in their lives is that it sounds too full of exhausting regimentation.

But structuring doesn't have to mean drudgery; in fact, the very point of structuring is to enhance your planning and therefore make room in your life for what you really want to do! You structure the *kind of life that is most effective for you* to reach your goals. And that life needs to include more than daily grind!

Let's consider some of the areas in a person's life that can be improved by structuring:

A Change of Pace. I find that I do better when I have a day set up with some change-of-pace activities. I can face a day with greater enthusiasm when I have some enjoyment or satisfaction planned along the way. I find that the toughest time of a busy day at the office (when I'm stuck to the chair too long) is mid-afternoon. I begin to slow down and get sluggish about that time of day if it has been a particularly sedentary day. So I usually build an errand into my plan for the day, a trip to the hospital to call on someone, a coffee break with a colleague. In other words, knowing that a busy day at the desk leads to sluggishness, you plan and look forward to varying the patterns. Get up and get out when that kind of change of scenery will do the most good.

Vacations and Travel. I am a believer in the importance of a structured vacation. Not that I know exactly what I am going to be doing on the third Tuesday of my vacation, but I do know—several months in advance—that I am going to be at the lake, or driving up the Pacific Coast, or camping, or driving a motor home. Why the structuring? Because I so much *enjoy the anticipation* and excitement of looking forward to and working out the details of such an event. Granted, this approach to vacations is not for everyone, but it helps me!

Time for Other People. Most of us like to spend time with other people and to meet new people. So why not structure a regular time to meet with people—to get together with old friends and get to know certain people better? When people are part of your plan, you can look forward with delight to spending time with them instead of thinking of them as interruptions.

This coming Sunday, for instance, my wife and I have invited three young couples over to our home for brunch because I want to get to know them and I want them to know each other. I'm looking forward to that time with them.

Books. I try to build reading certain books into my plan. And as a structure to help me achieve that plan, I keep those books right beside my desk in plain sight. Seeing that pile of delightful reading always makes the future look bright and interesting to me.

Schedule Tasks, Aspirations—in short, *life itself* is available to be structured so as to maximize the use of your time and energy and to help you arrive at the places you want to be.

Now, the important thing about planning and structuring is not that you should use the same techniques and structures as I do. My activities and situation may not be similar to yours, and I modify my system regularly as my circumstances change. Choose the structures that put you in control.

═══ *SUMMARY* ═══

Once you have a list of your goals, develop in detail the steps you will need to take to reach your goals. Share these steps with a friend or colleague. Flag the vulnerable spots where it might go wrong, use structures to assist you along the way for tasks, paperwork, time, reminders—all kinds of things. Plan your work, and work your plan. Plan your life, and live the plan—but be sure to make it well worth the while in the planning of it.

Much Obliged 9

So now you're ready to embark on a more affable, more confident, more effective life. Your goals are clarified, your plan is in place, and you're ready to spend some quality time accomplishing what is truly important to you.

But what do you do about that committee meeting you promised to chair next week? And the youth retreat you are scheduled to sponsor? And the shelves you said you would help your neighbor put up? And then there's your club meeting . . . the laundry . . . the charity fundraiser . . . the PTA—not to mention the lawn, the kitchen, and time with your spouse and kids. When are you going to find time in all that to act on your plan?

The problem that comes for many when they try to process their new goals into a plan is that they find they are already overly committed. Their schedules and their attitudes are firmly shaped and colored by previous decisions in life. In the words of Robert Frost, they have "promises to keep" and "miles to go" before they sleep. There are things they would like to do—but they are already obliged to do *other* things. They feel trapped by their past and obligated to the hilt. This makes life feel inflexible.

═══ *VARIATIONS OF THE DILEMMA* ═══

The trap of over-obligation can take many forms. Some people simply have taken on *too many commitments* because they never know when to say "No." They belong to too many worthy organizations and have taken upon themselves too many good causes. And as a result they are running in too many directions.

132

Others can't distinguish between real, legitimate obligations and imagined ones. Without distance or perspective about their commitments, they find themselves in a welter of conflicting promises that overwhelm and baffle them. Their problem is *confusion*.

Some are involved in *competing* obligations, particularly within their families. Couples find themselves at odds with one another because they are not in agreement about *what* they are obliged to do, *where* they are obliged to go, and *who* they are obliged to give priority to. Or an individual is involved with various commitments —all clamoring for equal recognition, time, and energy—that compete with one another because she has not spelled out to her own satisfaction which has priority.

And then there are those who have been *conned* by false obligations—sold a bill of goods by the deceiving world. In the Book of Romans, Paul talks a good deal about the tendency of the flesh—our fallen, sinful nature—to insist that we must be obligated to its entreaties. Paul points out that we have no obligation to our fallen sinful nature, which has so often ill-advised us in the past (Rom. 8:12).

ROOTS OF THE PROBLEM

OUR FALLEN INCLINATION

Where does the problem of over-obligation come from? This painful dilemma has several possible causes. Perhaps one of the most widespread causes is the one alluded to above—our fallen, sinful nature. Because of our fallen inclination, we do things that are bad for us—and that includes being over-obligated.

The pull of the flesh can lead us to over-obligate ourselves in at least three ways; all three can result in promises that fill our lives with stress and competition:

First, there is *inordinate desire*. We all have strong desires within us that are a part of our fallen sinful nature. They tell us that we must do this, we must do that—or we are going to be left out or frustrated. We feel that we will break out in a bad rash if we don't have this woman, this sports car, this job, and on and on. Because of these strong desires to have, to do, to be—we over-commit ourselves. We make promises we cannot keep because we have such a compulsive desire for more and more.

Another manifestation of our fallen nature that leads us into over-obligation is *exaggerated expectations.* Because we are prideful, we sometimes get grandiose, unrealistic ideas about ourselves. We want so to make ourselves look important that we make promises we cannot possibly keep.

Finally, because our fallen nature is often insecure, some of us develop a problem with our *people-pleasing tendencies.* We desperately need the approval of other people in order to strengthen our self-image. And so, in an effort to please everyone and to be loved by all—or to avoid offending anybody— we make too many commitments.

Jesus pointed out that if you set as your guide the pleasing of the crowd, you are on a path to doom. Jesus used himself and John the Baptist as examples. You may recall the passage in Matthew 11:16–19:

> But to what shall I compare this generation? It is like children sitting in the market places, who call out to the other children, and say, "We played the flute for you, and you did not dance; we sang a dirge, and you did not mourn." For John came neither eating nor drinking, and they say, "He has a demon!" The Son of Man came eating and drinking, and they say, "Behold, a gluttonous man and a drunkard, a friend of tax gatherers and sinners!" (NASB).

Jesus says that some people in his day could be compared to children who are trying to enlist their petulant friends to play games with them. The children call out to their buddies—"I'll play a flute, and we can dance. No, you don't like that? OK, we'll sing a dirge, and we'll play funeral procession." But they don't want to play happy games, and they don't want to play pretend funeral games. Like so many kids throughout the years, they say, "Naaah, I don't want to do that."

In the same way Jesus contrasts his ministry with that of John the Baptist. They came with different tactics and strategies. John was ascetic, living on locusts and wild honey. He abstained from alcoholic beverages and practiced fasting. And the rulers didn't like him. Then, in contrast, Jesus came and entered into the life of the people. Neither he nor his disciples practiced fasting, and he even made wine at a wedding. But the leaders rejected Jesus as well.

And so, Jesus was saying, you can't set your priorities by the applause of the fickle crowd. But we do, and this people-pleasing tendency often gets us into trouble.

PEOPLE WHO OBLIGATE US

It's not just the fallen, sinful tendencies in ourselves that can cause us to be over-obligated. Remember, we also live in a fallen, sinful world in which people will often try to get us to do what they want us to do.

We can be over-obligated due to the efforts of good, well-meaning people—people who do so much for us that we find ourselves obligated to them. Their agendas may be good ones—but they are not our agendas.

And of course not everyone who pulls us into obligations is well-meaning, and not every agenda that is pushed upon us is good! There are people who, if we give them the chance, will use us for their own selfish ends and attempt through guilt trips and other means to get us to do what they want. We can find this kind of manipulation in just about any sphere of life—business, school, home, or voluntary organizations. It is especially common in the marketplace, where people will use any trick available to sell us their product.

A common form of over-obligation involves family ties. We have parents or grandparents who have been good to us and made sacrifices for us. Now they need us. They who were once the generous source of strength and giving now make claims on our own strength and giving. This may take the form of their needing attention and/or physical care, or it may involve their ideas of how we should spend our lives.

My friend Russ Reid owns an ad agency and television production company. In his early years in Canada, he was active in local church youth work and in Youth For Christ. He was going full blast in his career, heading for some sort of full-time ordained ministry. And yet he wasn't happy in what he was doing.

Finally Russ realized that being in ministry was his mother's dream for him, not his own dream. His mother was a strong Christian woman, and he loved her dearly, but his breakthrough came when he realized he had to have his own agenda for his life. He couldn't live out his mother's dream for him—noble and well-meaning though that dream might be.

Now, I am not saying that we should abandon our family responsibilities! But we need to be clear about our motivations and our priorities. Jesus said some very disturbing things that shake us up about family ties. He said that there are obligations to others —including the household of faith—that must be put above our obligations to family. And there are times, he said plainly, when we must be willing to leave father, mother, and children, and head out for him. He even told one person to leave without burying his own father!

═══ SOLUTIONS—RELIEVING THE STRESS ═══

I would like to suggest some guidelines for relieving the stress of being over-obligated.

CLARIFICATION OF OBLIGATIONS

We've talked a lot in this book about clarification. Whenever a person tries to straighten out his or her life, one of the most fundamental things that must be done is to clarify just what is going on —to sketch out clearly in his or her mind the full dimensions of the issue. Specifically, to clarify one's obligations means to draw some distinctions between real and imaginary obligations and to pinpoint exactly where the obligations come from.

Clarifying obligations can involve such things as listing current obligations, analyzing and describing them, lifting them up and turning them around, assessing them, appraising them, weighing them—sorting out the real from the imaginary, the good from the bad, the helpful from the destructive.

EVALUATING AND CHOOSING

The crucial next step is to prioritize your obligations, to choose which are most important, to say to yourself, "This promise takes precedence over the other."

This step is especially crucial because the obligation that seems most urgent is not necessarily the one that is most important. In the heat of the battle it is sometimes easy to lose sight of what you're really trying to do. To paraphrase the old adage, "When you're up to your navel in alligators, it's hard to remember that you're there to drain the swamp."

It is the responsibility of mature people carefully to weigh all obligations—considering which ones they might have committed themselves to in a rash moment—and choosing which obligations are truly the most important.

CONSOLIDATION AND CUTTING

After making some assessments and hard choices, you may see you need to make consolidations and even backtrack a little. You may need to take the hard step of cutting some of the dead-wood obligations out of your life.

Jesus teaches a good deal in the Gospel of John about pruning —stressing that the vine which produces much fruit is the one which has been radically pruned to get rid of the nonproducing shoots and branches:

> I am the true vine, and my Father is the vinedresser. Every branch of mine that bears no fruit, he takes away, and every branch that does bear fruit he prunes, that it may bear more fruit (John 15:1–2).

During World War II, one of my occasional jobs was to go over to my Uncle Henry's greenhouse in south Seattle and work on his hothouse tomato plants. Uncle Henry would pay me and my cousins Annie and Judy to go through the greenhouse and snap the "suckers"—the extra shoots—off the plants so those plants would produce big, luscious tomatoes—not just lots of luxuriant leaves.

If you raise tomatoes or if you're making life commitments, you'll get more and better fruit if you snip away the suckers that specialize in only producing leaves, not fruit.

CONFRONT—CONFESS—COMMUNICATE

Then comes one of the toughest parts—confronting yourself or significant others in your life about the insights you have come to.

This can involve times of prayer, asking God to help you deal honestly and healthily with your commitments. It may mean talking seriously to a counselor or a friend who can help you sort out your feelings so that you can face yourself or others. You may have to write some letters or talk to some people you've been avoiding. But the time comes when you need to confront the issue of over-obligation squarely, in whatever way makes sense.

You must confess, "Here's what I've been doing. Here's how I've stuck my head in the noose. I've made and implied and assumed promises beyond my ability to fulfill them. Here's how I've let myself and you down. Now I have reassessed my situation and I think I need to prune this matter out of my life. I need you to help me by releasing me from this hasty commitment I made."

You must make, as Alcoholics Anonymous puts it—a serious moral inventory. You must look the facts—and yourself—squarely in the eye, name the dreaded realities, and deal with them.

=== TAKING OUR PROMISES SERIOUSLY ===

Lest we prune our promises too quickly and casually, however, we need to note that the Bible teaches us to take promises—especially vows to God—very seriously.

We read in Deuteronomy 23:21 (and this emphasis is reiterated in Ecclesiastes 5:4–6):

> When you make a vow to the Lord your God, you shall not be slack to pay it; for the Lord your God will surely require it of you, and it would be sin in you. But if you refrain from vowing, it shall be no sin in you. You shall be careful to perform what has passed your lips, for you have voluntarily vowed to the Lord your God what you have promised with your mouth.

If you have made specific, intentional vows—be prepared to deal with them with integrity. Not to be true to your word is a serious matter; it is a sin. (A good resource on this issue is *Caring and Commitment*, by Lewis Smedes.*)

Being true to your word is one of the foundation stones of civilized life. Even the airlines are getting fussy about dealing with the problem of unused reservations. I noticed an article in the paper last year that one airline was offering an eighty-nine dollar flight from San Francisco to New York. But there were restrictions: It had to be round trip, and the ticket price was *not refundable*. More and more airlines are saying things like this. It's tough to run an airline, or a world, with people who make promises, but then don't deliver.

What do you do to get out of the bind of over-obligation while maintaining your integrity? The problem is to find a balance. There may be some promises you simply have to fulfill—perhaps you can ask for a time extension on their fulfillment. You may have to go to some people and ask to be released from your promises.

*(San Francisco: Harper & Row, 1988).

Tell them the truth—that you made your commitment rashly—and ask if they will forgive you and release you.

All this must be done diplomatically and thoughtfully—going back on a promise could damage a reputation or a friendship. I have found that at such times it can be helpful to call in a third party to counsel you and perhaps serve as a go-between if needed.

In all of this, the most important element is not to make additional irresponsible promises you cannot fulfill—they will throw sludge or sand in your gear box and make your life more apt than ever to "lock up."

═══ AN OVERRIDING OBLIGATION ═══

Perhaps the most helpful thing you can do to deal with a problem of over-obligation is to become clear about your central life commitment. If you were to take a hard and close look at your most central and vital life compulsion, the deep things that motivate you—what would it reveal?

The apostle Paul, after he met Christ on the road to Damascus, had an *overriding, lifelong obligation* that he spoke about on a number of occasions—an obligation to preach the gospel to both Gentile and to Jews, but especially to Gentiles, and to testify to the Good News—the gospel—of the grace of God. It was this overarching obligation that determined all the other obligations of his life.

In Acts 20, we find a moving scene that occurred while Paul was in the middle of his third missionary journey. He was on his way toward Jerusalem, and he knew he was heading into a tough situation there. So while he was at Miletus, just a few miles south of Ephesus, he called for the elders at Ephesus to come and visit him. Paul believed he would not likely be seeing the Ephesians any more, and he had some hard and tender things he wanted to say to them:

> And now, behold, I am going to Jerusalem, bound in the Spirit, not knowing what shall befall me there; except that the Holy Spirit testifies to me in every city that imprisonment and afflictions await me. But I do not account my life of any value nor as precious to myself, if only I may accomplish *my course* and *the ministry which I received* from the Lord Jesus, to testify to the gospel of the grace of God (Acts 20:22–24, emphasis mine).

Paul was an example of a man with a mission—a powerful sense of obligation that led, motivated, and compelled him to do the things he did, go the places he went, and endure the persecutions he put up with. All other commitments had to be weighed, examined, scrutinized in the light of this prior obligation to serve Jesus Christ by sharing the good news of the gospel of grace.

First Corinthians 9:16 summarizes that all-encompassing obligation: "For if I preach the gospel, I have nothing to boast of, for I am *under compulsion;* for woe is me if I do not preach the gospel" (NASB, emphasis mine). Paul's entire life was of one piece—and as a result he never had a problem with over-obligation.

A LIFE-ORIENTING COMMITMENT

If you were to list the ways that people today view their lives— what would you say is at the commitment center for most of them? For some it is a power compulsion, for others it might be approval, comfort, safety—or simply keeping their heads above water. For some it is family. I'm sure we could come up with a long list of possible life-orienting commitments. For how many would it be to honor God, or serve him, or share the love of Jesus Christ?

We are instructed in Colossians 3:1 to "set our minds on things that are above, where Christ is, seated at the right hand of God."

Gordon Cosby, well known as the pastor of the Church of the Saviour in Washington, D.C., was—many years ago—the pastor of a small Baptist Church outside of Lynchburg, Virginia. One day a deacon in that church shared a concern with him. It seems that in their church was a very poor widow with six children. The deacons had discovered she was giving a tiny pittance—a few dollars each month—to the church, a tithe of her small income. She was so poverty-stricken that the deacons felt she couldn't afford to give even this much. They decided the pastor should call on her and assure her that they understood her circumstances and felt she was under no obligation to give anything to the church.

Cosby relates the story: "I am not wise now, I was less wise then. I went and told her of the concern of the deacons. I told her as graciously and as supportively as I knew how that she was relieved of the responsibility of giving. As I talked with her . . . tears came to her eyes. 'I want to tell you,' she said, 'that you are taking away the last thing that gives my life dignity and meaning.'"

That woman had a commitment to Christ that was at the heart of her life. For her, *giving* was deeply symbolic of that commitment. To ask her not to give was to ask her to give up the core of her faith and devotion.

HINDSIGHT

For some of us—this business of discovering an overarching obligation in life is something we don't discover right away; it emerges en route through our lives. We get smarter with hindsight. Some of us look back on our lives and see that while we were working furiously with one end in mind, God was busy at work in us for other purposes. And then one day, looking over the pattern of our lives we say: "OK, Lord, I see it now." What we had earlier resisted, we now see as a good pattern that God has allowed.

You may have read Brian Garfield's book, *The Paladin*, which is subtitled "A Novel Based on Fact." It purports to tell the true story of a young Englishman named Christopher Creighton. The story starts with ten-year-old Christopher climbing over a newly built brick wall, which tumbles down with him in a heap because the mortar has not yet hardened. And so the young boy falls unceremoniously into the presence of the middle-aged fat man who had just put up the wall—and, worse, happens to be his landlord. With such an inauspicious beginning, young Chris made the acquaintance of Winston Churchill.

The book, which I commend to you, grows into an exciting story in which the young boy becomes a fifteen-year-old spy against the Germans. Throughout the Second World War he acts as a special secret agent of Churchill. The book leads to a thrilling climax as Christopher is deliberately sent into a trap behind enemy lines. The boy, of course, doesn't know it is a trap. Churchill knows the boy will be caught and tortured and will reveal all that he knew about the planned Allied landing on the continent on D-Day. And Chris has been told the truth—that the landings would be at Normandy, not Calais. But the British also know that the Germans would never believe such a vulnerable young spy would be entrusted with the truth and so would be sure that the Allies would land at Calais.

Christopher is set apart for service in great trials of pain—to accomplish a task that was greater than he was, a task even greater than his friend, former landlord, and Prime Minister, Winston Churchill. And he lives to confront the Prime Minister. He says to Churchill, "You shopped me, Sir." Churchill says, "Yes, I did," and then explains his motive and asks his forgiveness. The Prime Minister says, "You broke under intolerable pressure, and you must feel great shame and guilt for that. I can only tell you that the shame and the guilt are mine. You betrayed no one. We knew you would break. We depended on it. No man every born on this planet could have withstood more than you withstood." When Christopher has digested this, the Prime Minister says, "Are you still with me?" And the young man replies, "I'm still with you, sir."*

This may seem like a hard story. We hate to think of a great man allowing someone who had been like a son to him to be deceived and trapped. And yet, God sent his own Son, Jesus Christ, into a trap—of sorts. And Christ was cruelly crucified. He cried out on the cross, "My God, My God, Why hast thou forsaken me?" (Mark 15:34). At that moment he felt what it was like to be sacrificed for a cause.

And yet, it was Christ's willingness to be caught in the web and guilt of sin and bear its brunt that vouchsafed our salvation—"With his stripes we are healed" (Isa. 53:5).

═══ THE VOWS OF GOD ARE UPON ME ═══

Are you willing for your life to be obligated, promised, used—for something larger than your own life? A hard question, indeed! But this is the stuff of which a truly winning life is made.

Jim Elliot, one of the five missionaries who eventually were martyred by the Auca Indians in 1956, evidenced such a strong sense of call when he was making plans to go into missionary service in Ecuador. He wrote to friends who had encouraged him to consider ministry in the United States where many needed a deeper understanding of the Bible's truth. Here are his words—strong and almost strident in their zeal:

> I dare not stay home while Quichuas perish. What if the well-filled church in the homeland needs stirring? They have the Scriptures, Moses, and the prophets, and a whole lot more. Their condemnation is written on their bank books and in the dust on their Bible covers.

Later, as Elliot sought a partner to go to Ecuador with him, he corresponded with Pete Fleming, who had just received his M.A. in English from the University of Washington. Jim Elliot wrote to Pete:

*Brian Garfield, *The Paladin* (New York: Bantam Books, 1979), pp. 3–6, 333–336.

I would certainly be glad if God persuaded you to go with me, but if the Harvest-Chief does not move you, I hope you remain at home. To me, Ecuador is an avenue of obedience to the simple word of Christ. There is room for me there, and I am free to go. Of this I am sure. He will lead you too, and not let you miss your signs. The sound of "gentle stillness" after the thunder and wind have passed will be the ultimate word from God. Tarry long for it. Remember the words of Amy Carmichael: "The vows of God are on me. I may not stay to play with shadow or pluck earthly flowers, till I my work have done and rendered up account."*

AMBIGUITIES—DRIVEN OR CALLED?

In Romans 6 and 7, Paul talks about being a *slave* to God (as opposed to being a slave to our fallen, sinful nature). In 1 Corinthians 9:16, he talks about having a *compulsion* to preach the gospel. In Romans 1:1, he talks about being *called of God* as an apostle.

Now, at first glance this variation of language can be confusing in regard to the various motivational compulsions that spark us. Are we to be slaves or free persons? Are we to be compelled—driven—or called?

Though there are not clear linguistic differences in the Scripture, I believe there is a clear psychological and theological difference between the person who is pushed or driven by powerful, unhealthy forces that may well be foreign to his central desires—compelled or driven in the negative sense of the word—and those who are *called*, invited, who freely choose to follow a certain direction in life. We have all seen the contrasts between the *driven* and the *called* in people around us—if not in our own lives. In one there is an emphasis on an abusive and hurtful slavery, and in the other there is an emphasis on a healthy freedom to choose.

Then what did Paul mean when he spoke of being both "slave" and "called." Og Mandino, in his marvelous little book, *The Greatest Salesman in the World*, clarifies the relationship between the two in one of his basic principles: "I will form good habits, and become their slaves."

In Mandino's book, the *freedom* lies in the voluntary choosing of healthy habits you elect to enslave yourself to; in such a case the slavery is healthy, voluntary, and potentially life-enhancing.

*Adapted from Elizabeth Elliot, *Through Gates of Splendor* (Wheaton, IL: Living Books, Tyndale House, 1984), pp. 19–21.

And Paul's point would be similar. We are called, and we freely choose, to give ourselves to God; we voluntarily make ourselves slaves to his purpose.

Such a voluntary choice becomes important for countering the "drivenness" of the flesh—sin's drive or compulsion against our better impulses. The most commonly cited source of this idea is Romans 7, where Paul contrasts the negative compulsion of sin and the positive compulsion of the new nature. As Paul writes in Romans 7:22, "In my inner being I delight in God's law; but I see another law at work in the members of my body, waging war against the law of my mind and making me a prisoner of the law of sin at work within my members" (NIV). *The issue is control.* In verse 25 he sums it up: "So then, I myself in my mind am a slave to God's law, but in the sinful nature a slave to the law of sin" (NIV).

How vital it is then that we have a strong sense of a call we have willingly chosen to follow! We are entreated to follow God voluntarily rather than simply being driven by the forces of our fallen, sinful nature—and obligated by our own pride and the manipulations of others.

If you are a *driven* person, however, freely choosing to make God your dominant obligation may not be all that easy. You can make a first step in that direction by giving to him your *willingness* to put him first. But then you may need to ask God—and perhaps a caring friend or qualified counselor—to help you along the path of clarifying and understanding what the source of *your* drivenness is. Then you can begin the process of letting go of your compulsions and answering God's call in your life.

HOW DO I DECIDE ABOUT MY OBLIGATIONS?

Beyond what Paul considered his primary, overarching obligation to God—he taught a seemingly paradoxical form of *minimal/maximalism* in the area of obligations. In Romans 13:8–10 we read:

> *Owe no one anything,* except to love one another; for he who loves his neighbor has fulfilled the law. The commandments, "You shall not commit adultery, You shall not kill, You shall not steal, You shall not covet," and any other commandment, are summed

up in this sentence, "You shall love your neighbor as yourself."
Love does no wrong to a neighbor; therefore love is the fulfilling
of the law.

It seems like a paradox. First Paul says, "Owe no one anything." He starts out sounding as if he believes in minimal obligations between people. If you stopped there you could read it,
"Don't get entangled with people. Don't make promises. Don't
get involved in obligations. Don't build up their expectations."
But then Paul adds, " . . . except to love one another." And loving people involves maximal, involved obligation.

But it's not really a contradiction. Paul is saying—*yes, be involved with people,* but not on the world's basis of excessive, formal, ego-involved promises, and not on the basis of manipulation
or coercion, but rather on the level of voluntary personal concern
—genuine agape love for one another.

Paul seems both to simplify and complicate the matter in one
sentence. And yet, the idea is essentially simple: your obligation to
people rests in the quality of person you are, not in what you agree
to do. Your obligation is to be a genuine person, even in your halt-
ing weakness.

Henri J. M. Nouwen hints at this principle in his book, *Gracias!
A Latin American Journal.* On the subject of living in a foreign
culture, such as Peru, the well-known priest writes,

> One of the most rewarding aspects of living in a strange land is
> the experience of being loved not for what we can do, but for who
> we are. When we become aware that our stuttering, failing, vul-
> nerable selves are loved even when we hardly progress, we can let
> go of our *compulsion to prove ourselves* and be *free to live* with
> others in a fellowship of the weak. That is true healing.*

If we take seriously the opportunity to be free and authentic,
and if we couple that freedom with a love of God—which Paul also
teaches—we will be guided by God and by the gentle entreaties of
our hearts as to just what our obligations should be. We won't have
a huge book of legalistic rules to guide us, but we will have a
tender heart—a heart that is informed and kept sensitive by the
Holy Spirit. Such a heart can make Spirit-directed decisions about
what our obligations are in each fresh circumstance of life.

*(San Francisco: Harper & Row, 1983), p. 17.

OBLIGATING OTHERS

Of course, the other side of choosing to be free and authentic is that we grant that freedom to others, too. Christians are not to be in the business of putting people under any kind of oppressive binding obligation; we are to lift and share burdens, not create them.

It is not our responsibility to coerce people into commitments. This is what the Pharisees did, and Jesus chastised them for it. Speaking of the teachers of the law and the Pharisees, Jesus said, in Matthew 23:4, "They tie up heavy loads and put them on men's shoulders, but they themselves are not willing to lift a finger to move them."

Paul understood this important difference between the approach of the Pharisees and that which was to be the role of the Christian, who was to bring liberation. In Paul's teaching on stewardship, for example, we see his emphasis on volunteerism and the freedom to make our own choices:

> He who sows sparingly will also reap sparingly, and he who sows bountifully will also reap bountifully. Each one must do as he has made up his mind, *not reluctantly or under compulsion,* for God loves a cheerful giver (2 Cor. 9:6–7).

The obligations and motivations of love do not seek to lay obligations on other people. As Nouwen points out further on in *Gracias!:*

> The more I think about the meaning of living and acting in the name of Christ, the more I realize that what I have to offer to others is not my intelligence, skill, power, influence, or connections, but my own human brokenness through which the love of God can manifest itself. The celebrant in Leonard Bernstein's *Mass* says: "Glass shines brighter when it's broken . . . I never noticed that." This, to me, is what ministry and mission are all about. Ministry is entering with our human brokenness into communion with others and speaking a word of hope. This hope is not based on any power to solve the problems of those with whom we live, but on the love of God, which becomes visible when we let go of our fears of being out of control and enter into his presence in a shared confession of weakness.*

*Ibid., pp. 17–18.

═══ SUMMARY ═══

To live a confident and affable life—in the best sense of these words—is to be obligated. Not with the stifling, draining proliferation of obligations exemplified in the fallen, pagan world about us. Not to be obligated in a slavery that oppresses. But, like Paul, to be obligated by an overarching compulsion to obey Christ and to be open, authentic, and loving. To be obligated is to love even in and through our weaknesses, brokenness, and vulnerability.

Toward *10* an Affable Mindset

If you have a computer with sophisticated data base software, you can store vast amounts of information. Then you have the option of setting a "filter" to tell the computer to deal with only certain kinds of information out of all that is available.

For instance, you can set a filter that tells the computer to only look for items that happened before 1983, or to look only for addresses that are in Detroit, or to pick out bills that are overdue. With the filter, you can be highly selective in what the computer brings to the screen.

This is also true in our lives. We can set a "filter" in our minds that will include or exclude, diminish or highlight certain kinds of input from the world around us. We can filter life to enhance it and make it more affable—or just the opposite. We do this by the set of our mind.

The Bible talks a good deal about the fact that we are responsible for the set of our minds. In Colossians 3:2, for example, we read: "Set your minds on things that are above, not on things that are on earth." And 1 Peter 1:13 says, "Therefore gird up your minds, be sober, set your hope fully upon the grace that is coming to you at the revelation of Jesus Christ."

We are responsible for our "filter"—for the way our minds are set. We can see the bottle as half full or half empty. We can see life as a pile of problems or as a hopper of opportunities:

> Life's little ills annoyed me
> When life's little ills were few.
> And the one fly in the ointment
> Put me in an awful stew!

148

But experience has taught me
The infrequent good to prize
Now I'm glad to find some ointment
In my little pot of flies!

Author Unknown

Consider some of the different possible mindsets that are available to us and which make life more or less affable. When Papillon stood on the cliff, he set his mind on freedom and escape. What are possible life orientations or filters that you could use?

═══ *WHAT IS YOUR CHARGE?* ═══

Remember high school chemistry? One thing you learned (or were supposed to learn) was that the atoms that make up all matter have an electrical charge. According to what was happening to them chemically, the charge could either be negative, neutral, or positive. Similarly, your "filter" or mindset can be negative, neutral, or positive.

Some people go through life with their filter set toward *getting even.* They are always ready set to pick up on the angry and hostile possibilities of life, and can be offended at the drop of a hat. Theirs is a negative mindset.

Other people are driven by *fear.* They have their filter set toward ways they can *escape or retreat* from life. They may express this negative mindset with alcohol, depression and anger, withdrawal, excessive TV watching—even through keeping busy with a hundred otherwise good activities that they use to protect them from dealing with the real issues of life.

I remember a "Wizard of Id" cartoon that beautifully illustrated this kind of negative mindset. The king is in the middle of planning a big battle. He has been told that the army is ready but that now they have to set a date to attack the enemy. So the king turns to the wizard and asks, "When's a good date?"

The Wizard says, "According to the stars, the third of next month is perfect."

After the king leaves the room, the wizard's assistant says to him, "What's so advantageous about the third?" The Wizard turns, smiles, and says, "I'll be out of town."

Then there are the people who have a sort of limp, neutral life focus. They survive; they go through the motions; they put one foot in front of the other, do the duty, talk the talk. They don't make waves. Their lives have no high points, and they try to avoid the lows. They are emotional zombies or semi-unconscious couch potatoes.

But gratefully, there is also the possibility of a *positive life filter* —where you go through life with your mind set toward a positive goal or aspiration.

It is this *positive life filter* that I would like to hold up before you, because that is what I believe God's Word would have us do. Your life will be more confident and affable if your mind-filter is set on positive.

A POSITIVE FILTER

Consider the mindset of the psalmist in Psalms 118:6–7:

> With the Lord on my side, I do not fear.
>   What can man do to me?
> The Lord is on my side to help me;
>   I shall look in triumph on those who hate me.

The Living Bible paraphrase of this verse speaks of an exciting awareness: "He is for me! How can I be afraid?"

And listen to the positive spirit in Paul's marvelous passage of 2 Corinthians 1:16–18:

> I wanted to visit you on my way to Macedonia, and to come back to you from Macedonia and have you send me on my way to Judea. Was I vacillating when I wanted to do this? Do I make my plans like a worldly man, ready to say Yes and No at once? As surely as God is faithful, our word to you has not been Yes and No. For the Son of God, Jesus Christ, whom we preached among you, Silvanus and Timothy and I, was not Yes and No; but in him it is always Yes. For all the promises of God find their Yes in him. That is why we utter the Amen through him, to the glory of God.

I have enjoyed reading Ross Firestone's book, *The Success Trip,* a series of interviews with people who are, by all the worldly standards we know, successful—people who have "made it" in this world. They are people from show business, advertising, the fashion world, sports, and politics. And in Firestone's book they all reflect on what success is like for them. It is both a disturbing and fascinating book.

One of those interviewed was Quincy Jones, who was the musical director for *The Wiz,* and a few years ago was involved in directing the *We Are the World* television special.

Jones tells about his attitude as a young man, when something inside wouldn't let him see anything as impossible:

> I just omitted every negative from my vocabulary, no maybes or can'ts. And I learned from those guys that when you get knocked on [down] you get back up, man, and dust it off and hit it again. I didn't get into personal trips with "this guy is trying to annihilate me from life" if he didn't accept my thing. You just keep on stepping, man. . . . But there was something inside that said, "yes, yes, yes," all the time. And so I would take any kind of negative trip that would happen, be it the unemployment line or being hungry or out of a job, and not let it turn into despair or escapism or bitterness or anger, but try to transform it into a positive energy. You know, put some notes on the paper, man, do some more records. The number one problem was that I wanted to write for the movies ever since I was fifteen and they wouldn't let any blacks get into that. So that part didn't have too much tangible hope in it. It took me seventeen years to do the first one. . . . But you just go with the flow. You know what your soul's about, and you just try to grow and prepare yourself and learn and get experience. Just keep on stepping.*

Your attitude makes an enormous difference in life. You can approach any task either with fear and anxiety or with a spirit of adventure and anticipation.

A year ago at Christmas my daughter Janeen gave my granddaughter Jenny her first bicycle. It was maybe a tad big for her—at least for a kid just learning how to ride. The moment of truth came when we went out to observe her first attempts. We went through the ritual of mother holding the bike in balance so she didn't fall. But eventually came the moment that Jenny tried to ride it herself. Naturally, she started to fall, and her mom caught her. I could see that the fear of falling could be a deterrent to the whole process.

So I told Jenny that one of the most important and exciting aspects of learning to ride a bike was the importance of mastering the art of falling. In fact, I said, what she needed to do was to *practice* falling—but correctly, without hurting herself. I told her that I would give her a dollar for practicing about a hundred falls. She haggled me down to a dollar for fifty falls. And then she started a very happy and positive game called "Practicing Falling Off a Bike for Fun and Profit."

*Ross Firestone, *The Success Trip* (Chicago: Playboy Press, 1976), p. 30.

After Jenny was well started in her falling program I went back into my study. Within ten minutes she was back in the house ready to collect for her fifty falls. I'm not sure if she is a truly *great* faller, but she certainly is a *fast* faller. At any rate, she quickly learned to ride the bike. And she had very few falls that led to crying, because she approached the whole learning experience—even falling down—as a positive adventure. She had a positive mindset.

Here are four positive mindsets I would like to recommend for developing a confident and affable mindset toward your life:

- Search for and discover life's hidden treasures
- Taste life fully and experience it enthusiastically
- Focus on belonging
- Focus on triumph and victory

SEARCH FOR AND DISCOVER LIFE'S HIDDEN TREASURES

Life can be an adventure of discovery. And looking at life this way is a much more affable a state of mind than seeing it as a tragic, depressing problem to resolve.

According to the influential psychologist and researcher Abraham Maslow, one of man's seven most basic needs is *to know and to understand*. And Maslow's work echoes a theme found in Scripture. The Bible makes it very clear that life can be an exciting search for the great treasures of life with which God has generously salted the earth (the italics are mine):

In Jeremiah 29:13, for instance, we read, "You will *seek me* and find me; when you *seek me* with all your heart."

In Isaiah 55:6 are the familiar words, "*Seek the Lord* while he may be found."

In the Living Bible paraphrase of Proverbs 2:3–4 we read, "Yes, if you want better insight and discernment and are *searching for them* as you would for lost money or hidden treasure, then wisdom will be given you and knowledge of God himself."

In Matthew 13:44 we hear the words of Jesus: "The kingdom of heaven is like treasure *hidden* in a field, which a man *found* and covered up; then in his joy he goes and sells all that he has and buys that field."

And Paul writes in 1 Corinthians 2:7: "But we impart a secret and hidden wisdom of God, which God decreed before the ages for our glorification."

I should point out that for the most part these hidden treasures of God are not hidden so as to keep us from finding them, but rather just the opposite; they are hidden *so we can find them* when we follow God's ways. God hides his riches like parents hide Easter eggs—so they can be found by even the youngest of the children who will give themselves to the hunt.

Many of the great stories of literature have been about a search of marvelous proportions. From the ancient *Epic of Gilgamesh,* in which the hero searches for everlasting life, to the medieval *Search for the Holy Grail;* from Henry Fielding's *Tom Jones* to Lord Byron's *Don Juan* and even Frank Baum's *The Wizard of Oz,* people have responded to the idea of a grand search. We even see this in our day in many of our movies, from *It's A Mad, Mad, Mad, Mad World* to Stephen Spielberg's *Raiders of the Lost Ark.*

What are *you* searching for in your life adventure? Are you searching for anything in particular?

I find that I'm searching on many levels. In my reading—which tends to focus on *biographies*—I'm always on the lookout for the fascinating, multi-faceted ways that people have lived their lives.

For the past year, for instance, I have been reading biographies of a number of the founding fathers of our country—men such as John Adams, Thomas Jefferson, Benjamin Franklin, and others— trying to understand the unique religious heritage of our country and how it has changed in modern times. But I've also been reading biographies of General Vinegar Joe Stillwell (*Stillwell and the American Experience in China*), Nuen Cheng (*Life and Death in Shanghai*), Tip O'Neill (*Man of the House*) and Arthur Miller (*Mindbends: A Life*). I find that every life story I read gives me new clues in the puzzle of what makes a person's life unique and successful.

LIVING WITHOUT DISGUST

To be a fully alive human being is to be searching. Watch a small child who—without inhibition—touches, picks up, turns around and around, examines, probes, and tastes whatever she can get her hands on!

A recent article in *Omni* magazine states that it takes about seven years for children to learn enough inhibitions in their searches to be disgusted with things. Actually, it is a kind of a fascinating (if disgusting) study:

> The fact that people don't stir soup with flyswatters or eat feces makes good health sense, of course, but disgust is the real reason

why they refrain. Disgust is a complex combination of taste, emotion, and cultural values that develops gradually through childhood.

And now the age of disgust has been determined, thanks to the work of psychologists Paul Rozin, April Fallon, and their colleagues at the University of Pennsylvania. It takes seven years of life experience, they found out, to become truly disgusted. Infants have no concept of disgust, and children under two, regardless of culture, will put anything in their mouths, from dirt to lizards. By age five, youngsters won't drink a glass of milk with a grasshopper in it, but if you take the grasshopper out they'll drink it readily.*

It's a good thing that we eventually develop a certain amount of disgust, of course, if only for health reasons. But how wonderful to develop discretion without losing that childlike drive to search, inquire, investigate—to have great curiosity. It is always exciting when you meet an adult who has been able to preserve something of that trait.

In the same issue of *Omni* I read an interview about a physicist named David Bohm. Interestingly enough, although Bohm has written one of the classic textbooks on quantum mechanics in physics, he has recently expressed grave doubts about this widely accepted approach. He is searching for an explanation of the universe that incorporates more than a discrete description of tiny parts and large forces. Instead, he has devised a whole new vocabulary to discuss the folding and unfolding of the universe as a continuous, seamless whole rather than an indeterminate collocation of subatomic parts.

To read the interview with Bohm is *mind-blowing*. It shows you a mind that is searching far beyond the narrow descriptive and mechanistic approach of so much theoretical physics. I don't pretend to understand fully what he is saying, but I appreciate that here is a man who is not content with the current models and is searching for a more meaningful way to understand reality.†

Too many of us have lost that searching sense of wonder—the wonder of the inquisitive child who has few inhibitions. Nor have we developed the sophisticated wonder of the questing physicist.

There is an amazing and wonderful world all about us. It is teeming with things to discover both within and beyond our reach. Fascinating people have gone before us and have lessons to share with us. There is a world of nature, a world of business, a

*Dava Sobel, "Continuum," *Omni*, January 1987, p. 28.
†Ibid., p. 69ff.

world of ethics, a world of personal relationships—all awaiting your discovery.

One day Marylou is talking to her mother: "I've been thinking about your hair, Momma. Have you ever considered dying your hair dark again?"

Her mother answers, "You're not serious, Marylou! I cherish my gray head of hair. It's like the mantle of experience. See this gray hair, Marylou? This is from the time that nice young doctor proposed to you but you declined because his specialty was dermatology and yours was that clarinet player. This gray hair is from your sweet-sixteen party when that motorcycle gang crashed the party—and how come they asked for you, personally? This one I got the day you said you wanted to share an apartment with three responsible roommates—Tom, Dick, and Harry. And this . . ."

By this time Marylou, totally stunned, walks out of the house, bumps into her friend, and observes, "I just found out how mothers keep score."

That's it! In your searching adventure, find out about people—what makes them tick, how they keep score.

I challenge you to make your life one of seeking and discovering God and the wonders that he has liberally scattered throughout his creation. Make it a life of seeking God's treasures in nature and in people. As Jeremiah wrote—and as Mendelssohn put it to music in his marvelous work, *Elijah*—"'If with all your heart ye truly seek me; ye shall ever surely find me.' Thus saith our God."

TASTE LIFE FULLY AND EXPERIENCE IT ENTHUSIASTICALLY

A second positive mindset for an affable life involves adjusting your filter and poising your expectations to *taste life fully* and experience it with vigorous enthusiasm.

The Christian faith is not just a list of intellectual dogmas to which we tip our hat. It is an experience to be lived—with vigor that we feel in our senses as well as our minds!

There are many appeals in the Scripture for experiencing God and his goodness this way. In Psalms 34:8 we read, "O taste and see that the Lord is good!" And 1 Peter 2:3 adds, "For you have tasted the kindness of the Lord."

For some people life may be dull and boring. Some may well be jaded and insensitive, cynical, unfeeling, depressed, withdrawn into emotional hibernation. They no longer experience life deeply, joyously, vigorously. But we are given the option of facing life as an experience that can be tasted and savored.

When you think of the idea of experiencing life deeply—what does it call to mind? That concept probably means different things to different people. We might list the following as aspects of life that are representations of feeling life deeply: euphoria, success, happiness, freedom, spiritual closeness, abundance, liberation, and surprise. Being in touch with sorrow and pain is also a part of experiencing life deeply. It is important to feel life's ups and downs as a fully alive person. A powerful and helpful book along this line is Harold C. Myra's *Living by God's Surprises.**

Such experiences are not necessarily good in and of themselves. Some deep and powerful experiences are harmful—if they represent drug abuse, infidelity, rebellion against God. We need guidelines to help us. We need to choose helpful experiences and nurture those which bring to our lives control, freedom, serenity, abundance, and accomplishment. And we need to discover how they fit into God's plan for our lives.

Take accomplishment, for instance. It is a powerful and good thing to experience the feeling of taking on a task and doing it well—tying it up in a bow, looking at it, and saying "That is done— and it is good. I did it!"

But tasting life fully also means being open to the experiences all along the way. As musical director Quincy Jones puts it,

> I always used to plunge into everything I'd do and I guess that's the whole point—to get an attitude from the beginning of plunging in and giving it all you've got, whatever it is. The same principle applies in whatever you do. And I was lucky that I always saw the difference between the hunt and the kill. I always knew that if you kept the focal point on the kill of success you really wouldn't get too much done, so I always found a way to enjoy the hunt. If I knew I had to walk across the park, I'd say to myself, I know where it is and I know I'm going to get there, but I might as well enjoy the pond and the birds and the trees along the way. You've got to enjoy what the trip is about because the success in itself as a final goal is really a false value.
>
> I didn't know that as much then as I do now, but I always found out if I worked hard and came home tired that I felt good inside and the reward took care of itself.†

*(Waco, TX: Word Books, 1988).
†Firestone, *The Success Trip*, p. 14.

That's one key to experiencing life fully: "Enjoy the pond and the birds and the trees along the way." Are you enjoying your trip through God's world? Are you tasting, experiencing, drinking life to the lees in the spirit of Ulysses of old? Noting the skies? Sensing the wind? Hearing the whispers and the thunders of life around you?

Jerry Della Femina, well known as the founder and president of his own ad agency, is also known for his book, *From the Wonderful Folks Who Gave You Pearl Harbor: Front Line Dispatches From the Advertising World*. In talking about his experiences on the road to his present success, he says:

> But there are successes and successes. Some guy could say, "Hey, I want to be a fireman." Because that's what the neighborhood dream was: I want to be a fireman, I want to be a policeman, I want to be a numbers runner. But I didn't just want to be a nice family man who goes to work at nine o'clock in the morning and comes home at five and earns a decent living for his family, and then they shovel dirt over the body and say, "Well, he was a nice man." That was not my concept of success. That's the only thing that was different about me from the rest of the people in that neighborhood. Me, I wanted to taste everything, see everything, do everything. I can remember when I was very, very broke, really broke, I guess I was about nineteen. I was just about to get married and was making forty or fifty dollars a week, and I would go into very expensive restaurants to eat and drag my friends along on the theory that some day I'm going to be able to afford great restaurants and I want to practice for them now. I remember blowing a couple of salaries practicing for success. That's how much I wanted it. I wanted even to prepare for it.*

Maybe God doesn't want you to splurge your whole paycheck on a fancy restaurant when you can't afford it—but he does expect you *to taste, to see, to do* — to be fully alive, fully experiencing your life.

A DISCRIMINATING TASTE

Now, it is true that there are problems, tragedies, and enigmas in life—and that experiencing life fully means experiencing some pain as well as happiness. But there are also glories to be sensed, realities to be reveled in. And as John writes in 1 John 3:2, the

*Ibid., p. 4.

glory we can experience in this life is just a foretaste of what we are yet to experience: "Beloved, we are God's children now; it does not yet appear what we shall be!"

But this awareness that there is more to come should enable us to be discriminating in our taste. Yes, taste life deeply and fully. But be sure that you taste the things that *deeply satisfy*— the best things, the healthy things, the things that wear well, the things that bring no regret. This not only will bring you satisfactions in this life; it will also develop your taste for the joys of eternal life.

Jesus is in the business of *bringing satisfaction;* he stated that clearly several times.

To the woman at the well he promised, "Whoever drinks of the water that I shall give him will never thirst; the water that I shall give him will become in him a spring of water welling up to eternal life" (John 4:13).

After feeding the five thousand he said, "I am the bread of life; he who comes to me shall not hunger, and he who believes in me shall never thirst" (John 6:35).

And in this life he gives us opportunity to develop a taste for— and an understanding of, an appreciation for—those things that truly satisfy.

═══ *FOCUS ON BELONGING* ═══

A third positive mindset—one that will help us toward more confident and affable living—is to focus on belonging. Consider the words of Paul in Ephesians 2:11–14:

> Therefore remember that at one time you Gentiles in the flesh, called the uncircumcision by what is called the circumcision, which is made in the flesh by hands—remember that you were at that time separated from Christ, alienated from the commonwealth of Israel, and strangers to the covenants of promise, having no hope and without God in the world. But now in Christ Jesus you who once were far off have been *brought near* in the blood of Christ. For he is our peace, who has made us both one and has broken down the dividing wall of hostility.

At the heart of the gospel is the idea of bringing people together. Here Paul speaks of the bringing together of Gentile and Jew. We are designed by God and rescued by Christ to live in covenant and love with one another. We are not designed to be hermits or enemies, living in alienation from one another.

This scriptural emphasis on the importance of belonging is backed up by modern psychology. In fact, Abraham Maslow, whom I quoted earlier in this chapter, lists belonging as among our three most basic human needs—ranking right after physiological needs and safety needs.

Psychologist Jess Lair, the author of several books including *I Ain't Well, But I Sure Am Better,* agrees that belonging is a fundamental and important human need. In fact, he has described what he calls "Mutual Need Therapy," which emphasizes, on the psychological and therapeutic levels, the absolute necessity of building personal networks. In order to be psychologically healthy, we must *belong* to some important and living circle of people—where we feel loved, important, safe, and wanted, and where love and caring are reciprocal.

People seek to meet their need for belonging in a great variety of ways. Clubs, gangs, fellowship groups, lodges, business associations—even the "regular" crowd at the local bar—all are manifestations of our need to be included, to identify with a circle of people we trust and feel secure with. (As the theme song from the television show *Cheers* goes, "You wanta go where everybody knows your name.") But the church—the Body of Christ—is God's fullest provision for that need.

There is a wonderful old story told about the Scottish pastor who noticed that one of his church members hadn't been in worship for awhile, so he called on him at home. It was a cold winter evening, and there was a fire in the fireplace. The man welcomed his pastor, and they sat by the fire quietly exchanging embarrassed pleasantries. After a few minutes of silence, the pastor got up, went over to the fire, picked up the tongs, took a red-hot coal from the fire, and placed it alone out on the hearth. As they sat for a while and looked at the blazing fire, the coal quickly lost its redness and had turned a kind of gray color. It had lost its fire and its glow as it sat alone on the hearth.

In a few minutes the man turned to his pastor and said, "I'll see you in church on Sunday." We need one another—to keep alive, to keep one another warm and glowing.

A marvelous mindset for a more affable life is one in which you focus on belonging to a circle of love within a local church—and I would particularly underline a small group (or what in our church we call a covenant group) as one of the best places to start.

160

BELONGING SKILLS

There are important skills involved in belonging and continuing to belong to a group: *listening* to people, *treating* them in ways that show we value their uniqueness, *communicating* in ways that show we care, and *accepting* people as they are without trying to pigeonhole or stereotype them or writing them off without getting to know them.

Admittedly, this takes imagination and effort. Networks of belonging are built by the act of loving and affirming people—but building such a network takes tact, work, and a lot of time.

We can practice these skills in our families, seeking to make them into effective circles of love. Fathers and mothers can teach their children; brothers and sisters, aunts and uncles can reach out, inviting one another to be in on a vital circle of love.

I learned this past week about one of our church members—a father—who makes it a practice to take one of his children with him on a short trip from time to time. One son went to New York with dad on a business trip. Recently one of the other teenagers went with his dad to Los Angeles, where they saw the Rose Bowl parade and went on the Universal Studios tour—and even made a music video to bring home for the rest of the family. What a way to build belongingness skills in a family!

We include people in a circle of love by cherishing them in individual ways. One of my favorite "Peanuts" cartoons shows Peppermint Patty, who is a rough-cut, tomboy kind of kid, opening up a long box of flowers. She immediately runs over and phones Charlie Brown: "Hey, Chuck, come on over, and see what my dad gave me for my birthday," then, when he arrives, points proudly at the flowers in a vase.

"Roses!" she says.

"Wow," says Charlie Brown.

Peppermint Patty says, "And you know what my dad said? He said that I'm growing up fast and soon I'll be a beautiful young lady, and all the boys will be calling me up, so he just wanted to be the first one in my life to give me a dozen roses." Then she adds, "He calls me 'A Rare Gem.'"

Charlie Brown observes, "Your dad likes you. Happy Birthday."

In the last frame Peppermint Patty is gazing at the vase of roses with a beatific smile across her face, saying, "Suddenly, I feel very feminine."

The sense of belonging, of being included, is a wonderful one. But it should be noted that there can be a dark side to the dynamics of belonging. As most of us are aware, the need to belong *can* result in cliques and exclusion. In other words, people join clubs and form groups because they need to belong—but then they keep others who "don't fit in" from joining! Also, the need to belong can lead people to go against their consciences in order to fit in. (A good example is fraternity hazing.)

The dark side of the need to belong is the tendency to exclude others and to do anything just to fit in. As Christians, we must be aware of these dynamics and pitfalls. And we must strive to keep the arms of the church wide open to all the hurting people who long so desperately for a place they can belong.

═══ FOCUS ON TRIUMPH AND VICTORY ═══

Finally, I would like to suggest a positive mindset that focuses on triumphing in life. A good theological basis for a triumphant mindset is found in 2 Corinthians 2:14:

> But thanks be to God, who in Christ always leads us in *triumph*, and through us spreads the fragrance of the knowledge of him everywhere.

So also the psalmist writes in Psalms 118:6–7:

> With the Lord on my side I do not fear.
>   What can man do to me?
> The Lord is on my side to help me;
>   I shall look in triumph on those who hate me.

And we see this mindset of triumph clearly in Romans 8:

> What then shall we say to this? If God is for us, who is against us? . . . Who shall separate us from the love of Christ? Shall tribulation, or distress, or persecution, or famine, or nakedness, or peril, or sword? . . . No, in all these things we are *more than conquerors* through him who loved us (vv. 31, 35, 37, emphasis mine).

We can have this mindset of triumph not because we are so great or talented, but rather because God makes it possible. As

Paul says in 2 Corinthians 3:5–6, "Our sufficiency is from God, who has qualified us to be ministers of a new covenant."

I believe that the Christian has the option of and the encouragement for a triumphant mindset for life—because we are on the winning side. We can approach life not as victims, not as martyrs, not as good losers—but as allies of the God who has triumphed in Christ and his partners in the unfolding of that triumph in history.

We have the God-given right to attack life with energy and vigor and joy. As one down-to-earth prayer phrased it, we have the right to go at life with "the determination and tenacity of a weed." That's a very appropriate image, for weeds never give up. They grow exuberantly, seeming full of confidence that they are going to win.

And they may well be right—as anyone who has battled them on his lawn will agree. In fact, a recent issue of *Smithsonian* magazine had a pictorial showing how weedy vegetation has won out over various historical monuments the world over. The moral of the entire layout seemed to be "You might as well give up— eventually the weeds take over civilizations."

Can you picture your life as one in which you set your mind on triumph? Can you understand the mindset of a victor rather than a victim? That kind of mindset comes through splendidly in the majestic closing lines of Stephen Spender's poem, "I Think Continually of Those Who Were Truly Great":

> Near the snow, near the sun, in the highest fields
> See how those names are fêted by the waving grass,
> And by the streamers of white cloud,
> And whispers of wind in the listening sky;
> The names of those who in their lives fought for life,
> Who wore at their hearts the fire's centre,
> Born of the sun they traveled a short while towards the sun,
> And left the vivid air signed with their honor.*

=== *SUMMARY* ===

What will be your chosen mindset for tomorrow and next month and next year:

- Searching for and discovering for God's marvelous treasures in life?

*Quoted in Louis Untermeyer, ed., *Modern British Poetry* (New York: Harcourt Brace, 1920, 1950), pp. 458–459. Copyright 1934, renewed 1962 by Stephen Spender. Used by permission of Random House, Inc.

- Tasting and experiencing enthusiastically the particular slice of life that God has given you?
- Focusing on belonging to God's family and including others in the circle of love and care?
- Focusing on triumph and victory—attacking life with the joy and the tenacity of a weed, knowing that you are the companion of a triumphant Christ?

It is for you to choose whether you will rust and atrophy or—by setting your mind in a positive direction—shine with use. As an encouragement to move toward the positive, I hold up for you the marvelous words of Alfred, Lord Tennyson from his poem, "Ulysses":

> . . . Come, my friends.
> 'Tis not too late to seek a newer world.
> Push off, and sitting well in order smite
> The sounding furrows; for my purpose holds
> To sail beyond the sunset, and the baths
> Of all the western stars, until I die.
> It may be that the gulfs will wash us down;
> It may be we shall touch the Happy Isles,
> And see the great Achilles, whom we know.
> Tho' much is taken, much abides; and tho'
> We are not now that strength which in old days
> Moved earth and heaven, that which we are, we are,—
> One equal temper of heroic hearts,
> Made weak by time and fate, but strong in will
> To strive, to seek, to find, and not to yield.

Learning Contentment 11

As we mentioned in the last chapter, we are each capable of putting a "filter" in our outlook—"setting our minds" so as to concentrate on certain kinds of attitudes and experiences. We are responsible for the set of our minds, and we can choose to *reset* our minds in a positive direction.

However, most of us start out with a filter already in place—we each see life through our own colored glasses that we have engineered over the years. We each have our own agenda, our own bias, and it is sometimes difficult to see things from any perspective other than our own.

One of the things pastors like to do when they get together is swap stories about professors they had in seminary—that is, the "Well, you should have had old Professor Dinklefuss" syndrome. They try to top one another with how tough the old prof was—or how strange, or idiosyncratic, or what-have-you.

I was involved in one of those sessions when a colleague told me this story about Professor Bruce Metzger of Princeton Theological Seminary. It seems that one day a number of seminarians were walking across the campus at Princeton when a squirrel fell out of a tree, hit the ground, and began a series of strange and unexplainable motions—apparently it was having some kind of seizure. The animal's contortions were so bizarre that several passers-by, including Professor Metzger, paused to observe its strange and erratic behavior. Then suddenly all the twitching stopped and the squirrel fell over dead.

At this, all were nonplused. They just stood there looking at each other for one of those awkward moments of silence. And Professor Metzger said, "Do any of you know the Greek word for squirrel?"

Yes, we all have our own individual mindset. And that was certainly true of the four ladies who were playing bridge in the recreation room of Retirement Villa—and also keeping a close watch on the traffic flow in and out of the rec room. A man walked in, and the ladies realized they didn't recognize him.

One of them spoke: "Hello! You're new here, aren't you?"

He replied, "Yes, I am. As a matter of fact I just moved in, and I was taking a little stroll around to look the place over."

Another lady asked, "Where did you move from?"

He replied, "Oh, I just was released after twenty years in San Quentin."

At this rather surprising turn, one of the ladies queried, "San Quentin? What were you in for?"

He said, "Well, I murdered my wife."

Immediately one of the ladies perked up: "Oh, then you're single? . . ."

Yes, we each have our own agenda, our own filter, our own bias, our own way of sorting through the experiences of life. We all have—to one degree or another—a certain amount of tunnel vision. But we have the possibility and the challenge of resetting our "filters"—to choose a mindset that sets us in a positive direction toward a confident and affable life.

So far we have explored four possible positive mindsets: (1) Search for and discover life's hidden treasures; (2) Taste life fully and experience it enthusiastically; (3) Focus on belonging; (4) Focus on triumph and victory. In this chapter we will focus on still another mindset—perhaps the most important to a truly affable life: a mindset of contentment.

=== A CONTRAST IN CONTENTMENT ===

Shakespeare's play, *The Tragedy of King Richard the Third*, opens with Richard, Duke of Gloucester, alone on the stage delivering a soliloquy in which he grumbles over his wretched state in life and his attitude toward his brother, King Edward IV. He is unhappy with his physical deformity and with the fact that the royal family all seem to be having a great time. He opens by alluding to "the winter of our discontent." He complains that he is "rudely stamp'd" and "curtail'd of fair proportion":

> Cheated of feature by dissembling nature,
> Deform'd, unfinish'd, sent before my time

Into this breathing world, scarce half made up,
And that so lamely and unfashionable
That dogs bark at me as I halt by them—. . . .
I am determined to prove a villain
And hate the idle pleasures of these days.
Plots have I laid, inductions dangerous,
By drunken prophecies, libels, and dreams,
To set my brother Clarence and the king
In deadly hate the one against the other;

Act 1, scene 1

Richard is clearly living in a hostile world—and he is not a bit affable nor confident about it. Richard has an enormous attitude problem. What others see as good times, peaceful times for fun and romance, he sees as a time to make an inventory of his problems.

In contrast—observe the opening of Paul's letter to the Philippians. Here's a man who also is physically afflicted—with a "thorn in the flesh"—and was in prison, but he's busily engaged in writing a letter of joy and encouragement to his friends who were out of prison:

I thank my God in all my remembrance of you, always in every prayer of mine for you all making my prayer with joy, thankful for your partnership in the gospel from the first day until now. And I am sure that he who began a good work in you will bring it to completion in the day of Jesus Christ. It is right for me to feel thus about you all, because I hold you in my heart, for you are all partakers with me of grace, both in my imprisonment and in the defense and confirmation of the gospel (Phil. 1:3–7).

And so we have two men: Richard III, who was angry and discontent because of the circumstances of his life, and the apostle Paul, who was contented even in the midst of hostile circumstances. What a difference! And what is the secret to learning contentment?

═══ BLAMING CIRCUMSTANCES ═══

Circumstances are the handy thing to blame when we are discontent. We all tend to do it. When asked why we are so miserable, we complain, "Well, let me tell you. Some guy bumped into my car, my secretary didn't come to work today, the computer is down, the check didn't arrive. Things are all screwed up. That's why!"

I certainly understand such circumstantial foul-ups. I drive a four-year-old Buick with over 105,000 miles on it. During the past two months, the transmission went out and had to be replaced. The engine threw a rod. The alternator took a hike. The battery went dead. And now the tires need replacing. These are circumstances that could bring on a mortal funk—and don't think I haven't rehearsed these items in the ears of my friends and colleagues!

We also tend to look to circumstances as the source of our *contentment*—or lack of it. In short, we act as if there were a direct, one-to-one correlation between circumstances and our attitude. The only trouble with such an assumption is that it's not necessarily true. It's not the circumstances that make the difference between contentment and discontent—it's how we interpret the circumstances.

We can see this most clearly by observing people who are in similar circumstances responding differently to those circumstances. For instance, Paul was in prison, and he wrote letters of encouragement. Henry David Thoreau was in prison, and he used prison as a place to challenge others, such as Ralph Waldo Emerson. Martin Luther King wrote a powerful letter to stir the conscience of the nation while in a Birmingham jail. Quaker founder George Fox managed to get people to gather outside his prison window and there he preached to them. Yet over the centuries, other people have come out of prison bitter, jaded, and angry. For them, prison was a school for crime.

Joni Eareckson Tada has used her physical disability as a springboard to international witness. And we could go on and list those who took difficult, even tragic circumstances, setbacks, and handicaps, and overcame them so as not to be defeated or turned bitter by them, as was Shakespeare's Richard.

Circumstances *are* important. They do make a difference, and given a choice, I'm sure we all would be inclined to choose the more convenient, pleasant circumstances of life. I would!

And yet most of us can look back to painful circumstances that ultimately proved to be a blessing, and for which we are now grateful. And we can look back to some easy circumstances, or what we thought were going to be greatly advantageous circumstances, that proved to be a snare.

When it comes to the relationship between circumstances and attitude, two mistakes can be made—and either one can mess us up.

The first is to act as if circumstances make *no* difference—the mistake of overspiritualizing the issue. Circumstances do make a difference. To deny that is to close our eyes to reality.

The other mistake is to act as if circumstances make *all* the difference—as if we can never be content unless the circumstances are perfect. Some people miss out on life because they have been overwhelmed or intimidated by the circumstances. Too quickly they say, "Oh, I can't deal with that; that's too much for me." And they give up.

Thus we want to be realistic about circumstances and not decide too quickly about which are a blessing and which are not until we have some 20/20 hindsight.

A couple of years ago, I heard a hospital chaplain tell the following story from early days in China. The story is called "The Lost Horse," and it is by Liu An:

A man who lived on the northern frontier of China was skilled at interpreting events. One day, for no apparent reason, the family's mare ran away to the nomads across the border. Everyone tried to console him, but the father said, "What makes you so sure this isn't a blessing?"

Some months later the horse returned, bringing in tow a splendid nomad stallion. Everyone congratulated them, but the father said, "What makes you sure this isn't a disaster?"

Their house was now richer with such a fine stallion, which the son loved to ride. But one day the son fell off his new horse and broke his hip, becoming lame. Everyone tried to console him, but his father said, "What makes you so sure this isn't a blessing?"

A year later, the nomads came in force across the border, and every able-bodied man took his bow and went into battle. The frontiersmen lost nine out of every ten men. Only because the son was lame and therefore not conscripted did the father and son survive to take care of each other.

Truly, blessing turns into disaster, and disaster into blessing: the changes have no end, nor can the matter be fathomed.

We make a great mistake if we invest too much or too little into the outward circumstances of our lives. It is only in time and with hindsight that we are more accurately able to assess the true role circumstances have played.

If therefore we determine that our immediate circumstances are going to be the key player in our contentment—we are hitching our peace of mind to the vagaries of life that surround us.

Rather, we should base our contentment on *who we are—God's children*, and how we are related to him.

THE SECRET OF
══ LEARNING CONTENTMENT ══

According to J. B. Phillips's paraphrase of Philippians 4, Paul says: "I have learned the secret of facing either plenty or poverty."

Paul had learned two things. He knew how *"to be abased"*: "I have learned the secret of facing . . . hunger . . . and want" (v. 12). And he knew how *"to abound"*: "I have learned the secret of facing . . . abundance."

The truth is that attitudes can be *learned*. We often assume that we are simply *given* our attitudes and outlook, like waking up in the morning with blue eyes—there it is, and you are stuck with it.

But Paul's secret lies in acknowledging that we can modify our outlook; we can gradually change our attitudes in the direction of contentment. Admittedly, this change may not come about instantaneously, but it *can* happen.

You can learn to face abasing circumstances in good ways or in destructive ways. You can learn to abound in good ways or bad ways. Both take education. What Paul is saying is that one can use wisdom and learning in either case.

══ WHEN CIRCUMSTANCES ABASE ══

What do you have to learn in order to be content when you are, in Paul's words, abased? Here's where we can profit from the experience of those who have gone through times of privation and humbling. Reading the lives of John Bunyan, John Woolman, George Fox, Polycarp of Smyrna, Corrie Ten Boom, Elisabeth Elliott and many others gives ample insight into the reality that contentment is possible even in "bad times."

As we study the lives of such people, we learn that God can use even difficult experiences to teach us, strengthen us, liberate us —to give us an experience of grace we would never have known outside of that abasement. A key to contentment is to look for the thing God has for us in the tough experience.

One of the most powerful books I've read in recent years is Charles Colson's, *Loving God*. It is a recounting of the fascinating experiences of people from various centuries. One of these people was Boris Nicholayevich Kornfeld, a Russian Jewish doctor who ended up in prison for a political crime in the 1950s, and whose story is a beautiful testimony of power and contentment in the midst of abasing circumstances.

While in prison Kornfeld became a Christian due to the influence of a fellow prisoner who loved Jesus. Even though as a doctor he had certain privileges the other patients did not—he was allowed to practice his medicine while in prison—he lived in the midst of suspicion, betrayal, and the constant threat of death from guards and the other prisoners. Still, the worse his situation became, the more he followed Christ. To him this meant to refuse to cooperate with the patterns of betrayal that were standard in the prison—he refused to sign the false documents that were required of him, and in effect signed his own death warrant by these choices.

Yet as the outward circumstances worsened, and the surety of his own death loomed larger, Kornfeld found a growing attitude of peace and contentment within his heart. The hatred and suspicion he had felt was lifted. The anger and violence in his own soul vanished. "He wondered whether there lived another man in Russia who knew such freedom."

Dr. Kornfeld knew his days were numbered, and he felt a growing need to share the marvelous liberating experiences that were his. He wanted to tell someone about this new life of obedience and freedom. (His Christian friend had been transferred.) And so one night he began to share the story of his spiritual journey with a patient who was awaiting cancer surgery. The doctor's ardor in telling the story caught the patient's attention, even though he was drifting in and out of consciousness. The doctor stayed on with the patient, talking with him into the night.

Later that night, while the doctor slept, someone crept up beside him and dealt him eight blows on the head with a plasterer's mallet. And though his fellow doctors worked valiantly to save him, in the morning the orderlies carried him out, a still, broken form.

But Kornfeld's testimony did not die. The patient pondered the doctor's last, impassioned words, and as a result, he, too, became a Christian. He survived that prison camp and went on to tell the world what he had learned there. The patient's name was Alexander Solzhenitsyn.*

*Charles Colson, *Loving God* (Grand Rapids, MI: Zondervan, 1983), p. 32.

A LARGER PERSPECTIVE

What can we learn in times of abasement about contentment? That often, in the long-range plans of God for our lives—there are far more important things going on than we are aware of at the moment. That we are the children of God and we have been chosen for strategic kingdom business. And that the circumstances we observe—good or bad, comfortable or uncomfortable, are *only a part* of the story. Someday we may learn what is really happening in our life.

After World War II, Corrie Ten Boom used to travel about and speak of her war experiences in Holland and her imprisonment at Ravensbruck concentration camp. She shared the story of God's love in her life—even through the truly tough times. (If you have not read Corrie Ten Boom's books, including *The Hiding Place*, out of which a movie was made, I urge you to.)

There were several things that Corrie usually mentioned to all audiences. She would take with her a piece of cloth with a crown embroidered on it. She would first hold up the cloth with the lovely embroidered side showing—all the threads forming a beautiful crown. This she would describe as the plan God has for our lives. Then she would flip the cloth over to show the tangled, confused underside—illustrating how we view our lives from a human standpoint. Corrie put it in verse, this way:

> My life is but a weaving, between my God and me
> I do not choose the colors, He worketh steadily.
> Ofttimes he weaveth sorrow, and I in foolish pride,
> Forget He sees the upper, and I the underside.
>
> Not till the loom is silent and the shuttles cease to fly.
> Will God unroll the canvas and explain the reason why,
> The dark threads are as needful in the skillful Weaver's hand,
> As the threads of gold and silver in the pattern *He has planned.**

A SYNERGISTIC STRENGTH

Synergism means working together in concert with someone or something else. In the Philippians passage on facing abundance and abasement Paul speaks of an empowering and synergistic

*From *Corrie Ten Boom: Her Life, Her Faith*, copyright © 1983 by Fleming H. Revell Co. Used by permission.

relationship with God: "I can do all things in him who strengthens me" (4:13).

As you face the problems of life, including the problem of your attitude, are you doing it all on your own, or are you using some of God's leverage? Are you bringing with you the resources and strength of a synergistic relationship with God to tip the scales in your favor?

We find additional clues to this synergism, this working together with God, earlier in Philippians 4:

> Delight yourselves in the Lord, yes, find your joy in him at all times. Have a reputation for gentleness, and never forget the nearness of your Lord. Don't worry over anything whatever; tell God every detail of your needs in earnest and thankful prayer, and the peace of God, which transcends human understanding, will keep constant guard over your hearts and minds as they rest in Christ Jesus. Here is a last piece of advice. If you believe in goodness and if you value the approval of God, fix your minds on whatever is true and honorable and just and pure and lovely and praiseworthy. Model your conduct on what you have learned from me, on what I have told you and shown you, and you will find that the God of peace will be with you (vv. 4–9, PHILLIPS).

This passage is rich in suggestions about how the synergistic exchange between ourselves and God works. Note a few principles here:

Don't Worry. Worry is a useless focusing over and over and over on negative situations without doing anything productive about them, without getting anywhere, without making decisions, just stewing and fretting in a nonproductive, endless circle. It is wasteful and unnecessary. And it is a decision—you can choose to do it or not to do it. Don't do it! Put God in charge of your concerns and your program of change.

Talk to God about Your Circumstances. Spill the beans. Dump on God. Let him know all the details of what is going on within you. Lay it out to him—what you think, what you guess, what you fear, what you feel, what you're angry about, what you're happy about.

Such prayer should be, among other things, a therapeutic catharsis with God. (Read the Book of Job and note the cathartic nature of Job's prayers to the Lord. They are loud and candid;

they don't mince words.) After all, God is always there, he cares, and he doesn't charge the way a shrink does!

No, I'm not saying not to go to a therapist or a counselor if you need one. But you can go first—daily, hourly, twenty-four hours a day—to God.

Affirm God's Peace. By faith, affirm regularly that God's peace *is* guarding your heart and mind (see Col. 3:15). Remember, he has his presence in your life. If you want to think of the peace of God as a guardian angel, do so. God is here, he is with you. Let him be in charge of guarding your mind and heart with peace.

Focus on the Good Stuff. Tune in your mind, your activities, your attention on the things that are true and honorable, just and pure and lovely and praiseworthy. Get your head busy with productive, positive, helpful, giving, outreaching things. Fill your life with "good stuff." Get busy with great things, loving things, people-helping things (see Phil. 4:8).

ONE WORD FOR CONTENTMENT

A look at one of the Greek words in Philippians 4:11 can be instructive here. The word translated "to be content" is the Greek word *autarkeia,* which comes from Greek ethical teachings and means "entirely self-sufficient." It means you don't need anything more. The word had been popularized by Stoic philosophers, but the Christians used it differently.

The Stoics taught that *autarkeia* was achieved by eliminating all desire; they said, "If you want to make a man happy, add not to his possessions, but take away from his desires." (Socrates used the word this way in his answer to the question of who is the wealthiest man: "He who is content with least, for *autarkeia* is nature's wealth.") The Stoics proposed to eliminate all *emotion* until you didn't *care* what happened to you or others. This was to be done by the exercise of the will.

Paul's use of the word is radically different. It indicates we can be content—self-sufficient—by an infusion of strength from Jesus Christ. "I can do all things through Christ who strengthens me." It is a synergistic effort—working *with* God, not just through exercising our willpower over our emotions and desires.*

---

*See William Barclay, *The Letters of Philippians, Colossians and Thessalonians,* Revised Edition (Philadelphia: Westminster, 1955), pp. 84–85.

═ WHEN CIRCUMSTANCES ABOUND ═

Paul says he learned to be content when circumstances "abounded," as well as when he was "abased." In Greek, the word for "abound" is *perisuo*—it means to cause to excel, to be in excess, to have plenty . . . and more than plenty. The interesting implication is that plenty, or richness, can be more difficult to deal with than want! But it can be dealt with in different ways, depending on our attitude.

THE RICH FOOL

We see one example in the parable of the rich fool in Luke 12:16–21.

> The ground of a certain rich man produced a good crop. He thought to himself, "What shall I do? I have no place to store my crops."
> Then he said, "This is what I'll do. I will tear down my barns and build bigger ones, and there I will store all my grain and my goods. And I'll say to myself, 'You have plenty of good things laid up for many years. Take life easy; eat, drink and be merry.''
> But God said to him, "You fool! This very night your life will be demanded from you. Then who will get what you have prepared for yourself?"
> This is how it will be with anyone who stores up things for himself but is not rich toward God (NIV).

Thrice Blessed—But Not Satisfied. The man in this parable owned land, and he had had a particularly good year in his agribusiness. By all common standards of life, he had it made—he was rich.

Riches are fascinating because they represent power, the ability to do things we might not otherwise do. I love the story about the elderly lady who was driving a big, new expensive car and was preparing to back into a parallel parking space when suddenly a young man in a small sports car zoomed into the space— beating her out of it. The lady charged out of her car and angrily demanded to know why he had done that when he could easily tell she was trying to park there and had been there first. His response was simply, "Because I'm young and I'm quick." When he came back out a few minutes later, he found the elderly lady using her big new car as a battering ram, backing up and then ramming it into his parked car. Now he was very angry and asked her why she was wrecking his car. Her response was simply, "Because I'm old and I'm rich."

Yes, we are fascinated with being rich because riches seem to promise both power and ease. Yet the man in Jesus' parable was obviously not content. He was a rich man and he had a good crop —so good he couldn't store it all. He had an overabundance, but he evidently wouldn't be able even yet to say to his own soul, "Soul, you have ample goods laid up for many years. Take your ease, eat, drink, and be merry," until he had safely hoarded all of his abundance into new and larger barns. Even though he was rich, he was still pursuing contentment—and in it all he was foolishly unaware of the transitory foundation of the kind of contentment he was pursuing. He had not learned to be content in his abundance.

Application. This is an *easy* passage for most of us to read— because we don't see ourselves in the equation. After all, we're not rich—not *really* rich like some, not rich like Hewlett or Packard, Sam Walton, Queen Elizabeth, or some Middle Eastern oil sheik— not rich like those appearing on "Lifestyles of the Rich and the Famous."

But compared to the standards of the vast majority of people on this planet, we *are* rich. By and large, most of us can't see our own wealth, we so take it for granted.

I don't believe for one minute that Jesus was talking about the super-rich, any more than he was only talking about farmers in Palestine who were short of barn space! No, the passage is speaking to *most of us,* not just a very select few. Jesus was talking about people who have it better than average, and who have had a good year in ways that involve much more than money. That means almost all of us at one time of our lives or another.

There are *young adults—couples and singles*—who are abounding in possibilities, in brightness, in family, in connections, in verbal abilities; in cultural, educational, and economic advantages that 98 percent of the world would give their right arms for. There are *middle-aged people* who are abounding in know-how, in understanding, in old-boy and old-girl networks, in connections, in varied experiences. And there are *senior citizens* who are abounding in discretionary time, in experience, in practical wisdom, in family ties. And yet they don't know they're rich! For many today, abundance still hasn't provided contentment!

There are *teenagers* who are overflowing with the treasure of youth, but who don't have a clue as to what advantages they have by being young and living in this culture and in this decade. Many of them are totally blind to their abundance. They only see the teen years in terms of the immediate problems that they are facing, and they feel impoverished.

There are myriads of people who are well supplied with good health, abounding in surrounding family nurture, in possibilities. Most of us are abundantly supplied with resources and opportunities and don't even know it!

Don't get me wrong. I'm not saying there aren't also *problems and tragedies*. After all, we're not in heaven yet. But I'm trying to give some perspective on the abounding resources that surround us and that we take for granted. Like the fish who is not aware of water because he's never experienced anything but water, we are inured to our abundance in life.

THE SECRET OF CONTENTMENT IN ABUNDANCE

How then can we truly be content when times are good? Contentment comes with a set of realizations that we need to remind ourselves of regularly:

First, be content by realizing how well off you really are. As the old song says, "Count your blessings!" In the midst of an affluent culture, we often count the *disparities* between ourselves and the super-rich around us and focus in on how poor we think we are by comparison.

Second, realize that lasting contentment doesn't come from the material blessings. They are nice, but they wear out. We've all known rich people who are miserable, and others who have fewer material resources but seem pretty contented.

Most of us who are over forty, now that we have the things we thought twenty years ago would really make us happy, find that we merely take those things for granted. We have no significantly greater sense of contentment with them than we did without them.

Third, realize that real contentment comes from knowing who you are in relationship with God—knowing that you are doing right, following God's guidance, and using his blessings as a good steward would use them, by investing them in people in need.

═══ *THE REAL SOURCE OF CONTENTMENT* ═══

Contentment comes from knowing that Christ resides within you—and that you are a fellow-heir with him of all of the riches of the kingdom. As Paul puts it in that climactic passage in 1 Corinthians 3:21, when he answers those who would find their strength and identity merely in parties of men: "So let no one boast of men. For all things are yours, whether Paul or Apollos or Cephas or the world or life or death or the present or the future, all are yours; and you are Christ's; and Christ is God's."

Contentment comes from knowing what is *really* yours—long haul, deep down, when push comes to shove, throughout time and eternity.

Our contentment, rich or poor, is dependent upon the ultimate awareness of the bottom line of our lives. So often we are living unaware of those great spiritual riches. You can have a more confident and affable relationship with life if you are experiencing contentment.

In west Texas there is a famous oil field known as the Yates Pool. During the depression this field was a sheep ranch owned by a man named Yates.

Yates was not able to make enough money on his ranching operation to pay the principal and interest on his mortgage, so he was in danger of losing his ranch. With little money for clothes or food, his family, like many others, had to live on a government subsidy. Day after day, as he grazed his sheep over those rolling west Texas hills, he was no doubt greatly troubled about how he would be able to pay his bills.

Then a crew from an oil company came into the area and told Mr. Yates that there might be oil on his land. They asked permission to drill a wildcat well, and he signed a lease.

At a little more than a thousand feet, they struck a huge oil reserve, giving eighty thousand barrels a day. In fact, thirty years after the discovery, a government test of one of the wells showed that it still could produce more than a hundred thousand barrels of oil a day.

And Mr. Yates owned it all. The day he had purchased the land, he received the oil and mineral rights. And yet, he had been living on relief—a multimillionaire living in poverty. What had been the problem? He did not know the oil was there. He owned it, but he did not possess it.

I do not know of a better illustration of the Christian life than this. The moment we became Christians, we became heirs of God, and all of God's resources are made available to us—everything we need to be the people of God, living fruitfully and leading others to God. But most Christians continue to live in self-imposed spiritual poverty—discontent—because they do not know how to appropriate from God those spiritual resources which are already theirs. Like Mr. Yates before the oil discovery, they live in ignorance of their vast riches.

All of those things are simple to say—and take a lifetime to learn to put in place in our lives.

In other words, contentment in bad times and good times comes from knowing you are laying up treasure with God all your life. The things you are doing now are your investment in eternity: "Seek first his kingdom and his righteousness, and all these things shall be yours as well" (Matt. 6:33).

We live in a world that only knows how to count wealth and resources in one way—by the dollar. Contentment comes from things that have nothing to do with dollars. Someone has written these words:

> I counted all my dollars while God counted crosses,
> I counted gains while he counted losses;
> I counted my worth by the things gained in store,
> But He sized me up by the scars that I bore.
> I coveted honors and sought for degrees;
> He wept as He counted the hours on my knees.
> I never knew till one day by a grave
> How vain are the things that we spend life to save.
> I did not know till a friend went above
> That richest is he who is rich in God's love.
>
> Source Unknown

=== SUMMARY ===

Paul said he had learned the way to be content whether full or hungry, in plenty or want, rich or poor. The rich man in Jesus' parable was not content, and he was totally unaware of the things that really mattered in life. Contentment can be learned as we seek to find God's meaning in all of our circumstances. Like Doctor Kornfeld in Charles Colson's story, we may be playing a strategic role in life rather than an easy one. Seek the strengthening of Christ in all circumstances. Leave the worrying to God, and rather affirm his peace. Paul was content because he was aware of his resources in Jesus Christ that made all other circumstances pale in comparison. That same kind of contentment can be ours.

Purge the *12*
Nonproductive Nonsense

You can have a more confident and affable relationship with life if you purge the waste—those things that devour your time, your energy, your focus, your attention, and that detract from your accomplishing the things you know are important and helpful.

It is an inelegant fact that a great number of people simply piddle their lives away on things that don't matter even to them, much less to anyone else. They spend their lives in neutral, racing their engines and going nowhere. They may convince themselves that they are doing what they really want to do, but deep down inside they suspect the truth and are angry at themselves and the world for the wasting of their lives.

═══ THREE KINDS OF TIME ═══

Time is probably what comes to mind first when thinking of waste —although the use of time also involves the expenditure of energy and attention. Let me tell you how I see my time, which I think of as falling into one of three categories:

PRODUCTIVE TIME

This kind of time is when I move smartly from where I am to where I want to be. It is the time in which I am able to accomplish my high-priority goals in life. When I look back on it, I can say, "That was an hour (or a day) well spent; I got something accomplished that was important to God, to others, and to me. It was productive; I was doing something that needed doing."

REGENERATIVE TIME

This a special kind of time—when I am doing something that effectively recharges my batteries so that I can function better during the productive times. During such a time, I am engaged in something that regenerates my body, soul, or spirit. It may be sleeping, walking, thinking, sunning myself on the porch, reading a good book, playing catch, going to a play or a lecture, eating out with family or friends, or whatever.

It is important for each of us to understand what those activities are (active or passive) that actually do renew us. Some activities do this for a certain limited amount of time—but then, beyond that time they cease to be effective. There is a law of diminishing returns with many of these—such as sleeping, lazing, eating, chatting, and so forth. They are regenerative only for a time, then they become a nonproductive waste.

WASTED TIME

This is all the rest of our time—the time taken up with doing things that neither move us toward our goals in life nor regenerate us. It is time spent doing things we regret, that drain us, that eat up our precious hours and days and prove to have no socially redeeming features.

Time wasting is an easy and natural happening. Peter Drucker points this out, noting that the drift to mediocrity is accomplished as a result of a "natural inclination to waste time, energy, money, resources"—in short, to waste life.

═══ MAJOR TIME WASTERS ═══

Here are a few generalities that can help you identify—and eliminate—the time wasters in your life.

THE COMMONPLACE WASTERS

The great bulk of time and energy wasting is undramatic and lost in the commonplaces of daily life. As management consultant Alec MacKenzie once said in an interview: "Most of us fritter away time we could be putting to better use for work or for pleasure." And MacKenzie believes that most of this waste of time comes from either an unreasonable fear of offending people or the failure to delegate or to screen interruptions.

He lists fifteen leading time wasters as follows (he is writing about a corporate environment, but his basic principles are helpful in almost any life situation):

- Telephone interruptions
- Visitors dropping in without appointments
- Meetings, both scheduled and unscheduled
- Crisis situations for which no plans were possible
- Lack of objectives, priorities, and deadlines
- Cluttered desks and personal disorganization
- Involvement in routine and detail that should be delegated to others
- Attempting too much at once and underestimating the time it takes to do it
- Failure to set up clear lines of responsibility and authority
- Inadequate, inaccurate, or delayed information from others
- Indecision and procrastination
- Lack of, or unclear, communications and instructions
- Inability to say "No"
- Lack of standards and progress reports that enable a manager to keep track of developments
- Fatigue*

An important part of cutting out waste is to be more aware of such everyday irritants and attempt to eliminate them wherever possible.

LOW-PRIORITY GOALS

If you have followed the progression of this book, you have already prepared a list of life goals. Let's say you have seventeen that you have ordered according to priority. One of the most common time wasters is to spend disproportionate amounts of time on items fourteen through seventeen. (The time survey you took as part of chapter 6 may have revealed a tendency to do this.)

A sure way to drift into mediocrity is to be overly fascinated with your low-priority goals. In fact, one of the important purposes of putting your goals in priority order is not just to bring to the surface the top two or three, but also to flag the bottom five or six, which probably should be cut back or dropped entirely.

---

*From "How to Make the Most of Your Time," *U. S. News & World Report*, 3 December 1973. Interview with R. Alec MacKenzie, p. 45–54.

Lesser ranked priorities are easy to slip into; they are appealing, but not as fulfilling or important as the ones at the top of your list. And sometimes they seem less scary and threatening, for the very reason that they *are* less important.

One thing that could happen when you analyze your priorities list to find this kind of waste is that a clearer understanding of your true value system could emerge. Some people value the "here and now" of experience; "Seize the day!" is their cry. Others value preparation for the future; like squirrels, they are constantly hoarding nuts for the coming winter. Thus one person may consider a weekend of skiing for the family a high-priority way to spend time and money because of the important value of developing family relationships while regenerating the mind and body. Another person might feel that the money might better be put into an insurance program for a later day. A third might see both as valuable and try to work out a balanced but compromised program where there is a bit of skiing as well as systematic saving for the future.

Another thing that might happen when you look at your priority list this way is that you might find yourself getting defensive about some things which are down toward the bottom of your list. You say, "Hey, those aren't a waste of time; those are really important to me. I don't want to cut down on those." Such a feeling of defensiveness could suggest that your priority list is really out of kilter. What you had indicated as your top priorities may prove to be only a form of lip service—a list of the things you think *should be* important to you.

This is another reason why goals and priorities should always be written in pencil with an eraser kept handy—and why you should "process" your priority list regularly—live with it, apply various tests to it, and periodically reprioritize your list if necessary.

The fact of the matter is that going after top-priority goals with enthusiasm and vigor will almost always mean giving up on some of the lower-priority goals. It's important to face the realities of that kind of trade-off and to make some decisive choices.

INTIMIDATION BY OTHER PEOPLE

Another common time waster is being intimidated into spending time on other people's priorities. We often let other people redirect our time and energy when they have no real reason or right to do so—we are simply too polite (or stupid) to bring it to a halt. We are *intimidated* into wasting our time on someone else's agenda.

This can be a difficult issue for us Christians, who sometimes confuse our mandate to be concerned about and love others with a tendency to simply be available for any and all kinds of people to pick our pockets at their convenience. I do not believe that letting others intimidate us into wasting our time is either biblical or Christian—let alone smart or responsible.

As a pastor, I find that an important segment of my time and energy must be at the disposal of people in need. But that does not mean that I camp on the sidewalk and put out a sign that says, "Please run my agenda and my life for me." That is not good stewardship of the time and energy God has entrusted me.

Jesus did not allow that to happen in his ministry. He chose twelve men as his inner circle, and he often went off on trips with them to focus on their training. He held regular "office hours," when he was available to the crowds—but *not all the time*. He frequently withdrew for times of prayer and rest.

We tend to be intimidated too easily by the demands and needs of others—even when we cannot effectively do anything to help them. People will come up and give us a book to read, for instance, and we are intimidated into saying, "Yes, I'll read it"—and then two weeks later they want a book report.

Avoiding the time waster of intimidation requires that you have a rather clear understanding of those to whom you are obligated, those you do feel right about letting into the management of your life.

The life of Jesus Christ is one of the stellar exemplars of not being intimidated by people. Frankly, Jesus was not even always polite in such matters. People would ask him questions, and he wouldn't even bother to acknowledge all of them—or he would respond by throwing a question back at them. Consider Jesus' response to the priests' and the elders' question regarding the source of his authority in Matthew 21. Instead of answering, Jesus asked *them* a question about the validity of the baptism of John the Baptist. When they wouldn't answer, Jesus, in turn, refused to answer their question (see Matt. 21:23–27; Mark 11:30; Luke 20:4).

The issue we come back to here is once again the issue of being responsible. Are you willing to be responsible for the management of your time? Or are you going to let any passerby take over that responsibility?

To be sure, there are extremes that can be taken in this self-protecting business, especially for those in the ministry. I have known some who (in my humble opinion) went overboard on avoiding other people's agendas. One associate pastor whose home was about thirty miles away from his church had an unlisted home phone number—and I mean not even listed in the church directory! Only the senior pastor and the church secretary knew how to get through to him, and he made it clear he didn't want to be disturbed at home. How and why he managed to pull this off boggles my mind.

I know a couple of other pastors who make it very clear to their flock that they do not want to be disturbed on their day off unless there is a death in the congregation or another emergency of that magnitude. In fact, one of these pastors has even been very abrupt and rude to the members of his church who have dared call him on his day off—and the members have smarted for years about their treatment.

I have a hard time with that, when pastors are called to servant leadership—and all Christians are called to be servants of one another. Still, each one of us needs to discover and build his or her own effective ways of not being drained by others—ways that fit within our situation and our understanding of the servant role of the Christian. After all, even the butler gets Thursdays off!

THE TYRANNY OF THE URGENT

Often the urgent or immediate things are actually trivial, but they so press in on us that we don't really get the time or the energy to attend to the genuinely important goals of our lives.

Say, for instance, that a former acquaintance from a town where you used to live hits town unannounced and just drops by the office. He'll only be in town one day, and he would like to have dinner. Now, you may have planned on visiting a friend or finishing a book—or just collapsing and trying to recover from a hard week. But this is the *only* night he'll be in town, so you end up changing your priorities to fit his.

Now, please understand that I am not saying having dinner with a former acquaintance is necessarily a waste of time! Ultimately, we all must define for ourselves what activities are worth our time and what are not. But we must all guard against the tendency to do something simply because it has *a time limit* or *demands to be done now*, not because it is truly important to us. It's like spending all your time answering the phone instead of working on an important project simply because the phone is ringing!

When we give in to the tyranny of the urgent, we end up always reacting instead of acting—letting the *most demanding* activities run our lives instead of ordering our own lives according to what is most important.

Sometimes the only useful response to "urgent" demands is a straightforward refusal to give in. In the situation involving the drop-in friend, for instance, the only positive solution might be a candid response: "Hey, it's good of you to look me up. But at the last minute like this I feel I have some commitments I need to attend to. I just won't be able to spend the evening with you. Next time give us a warning when you're coming through so we can be better prepared." (Of course, that preparation on your part may be precisely what they fear—you'll be out of town yourself!)

Now, admittedly, this candid approach doesn't always get great reviews by those who would drop into your life without warning or expect you to jump just because *they* are in a hurry. I know a couple of times I've used such an approach and was criticized to my face for it. But in the management of our time and energy, God has given us choices, and sometimes they are not easy or popular.

=== *SCREENING YOUR LIFE* ===

Jesus withdrew from the crowd from time to time so he could accomplish important things either alone or with his handful of disciples. Withdrawal was a way of *screening himself* from the crowds—of obtaining some time alone for prayer and spiritual refreshment. I believe that the judicious use of screens can be invaluable in helping us get our high-priority work done.

Even as I am writing this chapter, I have retreated again, this time to a generous friend's mountain home at Lake Tahoe, where I can take a few days for thinking, writing, and editing on this book. Writing is an activity that is important to me, but it is difficult to do while involved in daily ministry. In fact, I canceled attendance at an important convention to simply withdraw, to get away, to set a screen of over two hundred miles between myself and the daily press of life in the fast lane in Silicon Valley. My associate pastor will deal with most of the matters that come up while I am gone. And the church secretary and my family both know how to reach me if I am needed for an important matter. So I can concentrate on my work without worrying about what is going on at home.

Screens are plans, structures, or people which serve the purpose of protecting us from unwanted interruptions. They can take many different forms: a closed door, an answering machine, a helpful spouse, a trip to the country.

Sometimes even telling the blatant truth can serve as a screen: A secretary explains, "He's hiding out trying to get that report done which has got to be printed by tomorrow. Can he call you back when he's caught up?"

Sometimes using screens effectively means learning to hide constructively and inoffensively—and, I might add, honestly. I once knew a pastor who called his outer office "the office" and his inner room his "study," just so he could hide in his "study" and his secretary could tell people he wasn't in the "office" that day. No matter how you slice it—I call that devious baloney! But some hiding is essential for anyone who wants to do serious work on high-priority goals.

Elton Trueblood speaks of this in his autobiography, *While It Is Day:*

> A public man, though he is necessarily available at many times, must learn to hide. If he is always available, he is not worth enough when he *is* available. I once wrote a chapter in the Cincinnati Union Station, but that was itself a form of hiding because nobody knew who the man with the writing pad was. Consequently nobody approached me during five wonderful hours until the departure of the next train for Richmond. We must use the time which we have because even at best there is never enough.*

SCREENING WITH TACT

It should go without saying, of course, that screens must be employed with tact and sensitivity, judicious care and class. But some people manage to offend other people unnecessarily in the process of screening out interruptions.

How would you feel if you called up a friend and his wife or secretary or child said, "I'm sorry; he's not talking to anyone today"? Most people would feel the same—rebuffed and offended. But if you called and were are told that your friend was out of town for a couple of days, or out of the office for an hour, you wouldn't feel the same sense of personal rejection.

Somehow our culture has trained us all to be considered available if we are geographically handy. So, for many, the only way to hide without ruffling feathers is to leave town or go to some unavailable place (public library, park, motel, or a friend's vacation house).

*Elton Trueblood, *While It Is Day*, (New York: Harper & Row, 1974), p. 67.

In a home or an office, it is important for us to train those who screen for us in ways that protect us from frivolous intrusions when we are working on strategic tasks. Somehow it comes across better when a secretary says, "I'm sorry, Jim is unavailable just now, but if you will leave a message, I will be happy to see that he gets it when he is available" than for her to say, "He's too busy with important things to talk to you. Are you sure it's important?" And of course, if we are "screening" for another person, we need to be aware of the tactics that are less offensive.

PRESERVING RELATIONSHIPS

In speaking of using screens, the objection might be raised, "But if you set up all of these screens so that people can't get to you—what about the importance of human relations? Aren't you going to be destroying something valuable by erecting screens?" This is a legitimate concern, but as Trueblood says, the purpose of using screens is to be worth *more* to other people when you *are* available.

As Christians, of course, we need to be sensitive to the needs of people around us. So these protective barriers cannot be up all the time, nor should they all be impersonal.

One of the most helpful kind of screens, for example, is another person—a spouse, a secretary, a roommate. My wife knows that I am always available for real needs, and to specific people for whom I am particularly responsible. So does my secretary.

In other words, one of the hard decisions we must make is that we are more available and responsible to some people than we are to others. I am committed to the notion of *selective investment* of my life. The oft-quoted satirical slogan from George Orwell's *Animal Farm*—"All animals are equal, but some are more equal than others"—applies on a practical level to the need for doing this. It's a simple fact that some people—including family, colleagues, disciples, close friends—are strategically more important parts of my life than others. For these the door is more readily open; they are our beloved community.

The life of Jesus exemplified a marvelous balance between time with the multitudes, time alone, and time with the Twelve. Each kind of time was important, but the amount of time he spent in each was determined by his strategic plan of salvation. He spent more time with Peter, James, and John than the other nine. He spent more time with the twelve than with the masses. He spent more time with the responsive ones in the multitude than with the unresponsive—or with the establishment elite or the cultural despisers. He spent more time in Galilee and Judea than he did in Phoenicia or Gaza.

A TIME TO BE AVAILABLE

Another important thing to remember about hiding is that these times of being unavailable should represent only a portion of our time. A good deal of the time, my door and my life are open; I am available to one and all. In my mind, it is not acceptable for a follower of Christ to *live* behind a screen or a closed door like Howard Hughes.

I was impressed with something Mayor Tom Bradley of Los Angeles did when he first took office a number of years back. About once a month, he set aside a day when he was open, on a first-come, first-served basis, to chat with any citizen of the city who wanted to see him. People would line up to spend a few minutes with the mayor and air their concerns. Now, Mayor Bradley only did this one day a month, but it was a great opportunity to let people know he was not trying to shield himself arbitrarily from his constituents.

The answer to the dilemma of screening without offending or hurting relationships is once again to be found in balance—in not going to extremes. In each of our lives there must be time with God alone, time with friends, and time with colleagues, as well as some time with a broad range of people.

═══ THE PRINCIPLE OF SELECT AND PURGE ═══

There are many techniques for avoiding waste of our time and energy so we can focus on our high-priority goals. But almost all of these techniques can be boiled down to a single principle: Select and purge.

In other words, avoiding waste means you have to select judiciously *what* you will do, *when* you will do it, and *to whom* you will give your time, energy, and resources. It means you will purge out the dross and focus on the important. This takes intestinal fortitude and good planning.

Some time back I read an interview with actress Martha Scott. When asked about the great amount of energy it takes to rehearse and then act, she said,

> It's also exhausting. It takes enormous energy and stamina, much more than meets the eye. Once I asked Lucy Ball how she

could work 13 hours a day as a performer in television and also function as a producer behind the scenes. She said, "Get plenty of rest. Save your energy. Whenever you can sit, sit. Don't spread yourself thin with social activity." . . . It was a professional, real-life extension of something I'd first heard as a college girl acting in school plays. Our theater arts director wouldn't even let me go to a football game. Our school was very big on football, but when I mentioned going to the game, he really chewed me out. He said, "If you're serious about acting, you'd better know it's like taking the veil in church. You give up other pleasures. You can't use your vocal chords at a football game Saturday afternoon and expect to have a speaking voice Saturday night on the stage." In effect, life is a matter of choices on the road to a goal.*

This is a vital truth that is so often undiscovered or ignored in our "Jack-of-all-trades and master-of-none" culture. We believe so much in the broad democratic and uncritical approach to life, we often fail to recognize that to excel and reach our goals in a given area may mean something good (but of lower priority) has to be purged from our lives. There needs to be some narrowing in our lives if we are going to be able to meet our high-priority goals.

PURGING TIME WASTERS IN A HOME SETTING

When I have taught a seminar on Managing Your Life and discussed this matter of purging waste, I have often been asked how these principles apply to nonoffice situations—particularly that of the homemaker or the housewife. Not everyone has a secretary (or a wife!) to run interference for him or her. How does the domestic engineer protect herself from interruptions and set aside time to work on high-priority goals? Or how would a person who has chosen to work at home keep from wasting time?

Obviously, some of the mechanics and details will be different, but the principles remain essentially the same. Here are some ideas:

THE PHONE

If you need to get something done without telephone interruptions, there are several things you can do: take it off the hook or

Los Angeles Times Home magazine, 25 July 1976, p. 39.

unplug it, refuse to answer, or—best of all—invest in an answering machine. For a relatively small price you can have the capability of easily monitoring incoming calls so that you only pick up those you want to deal with at the moment. Besides, you won't miss any messages while you are away!

It is amazing, however, how much emotional discomfort many people feel over any assertion that you might ignore the ringing of a phone. Many people have told me it would be impossible for them to do that. The amazing thing is that people often treat incoming calls as if they had an overwhelming validity and power. And yet, if telephone calls are so important to these people, why don't they have someone sitting by their phone twenty-four hours a day to catch all of them when they are gone? When we are in the room with a ringing phone we tend to be intimidated by it. That we should think otherwise is a totally novel idea to most people.

I remember the story of Ed Toms who was deep in a conversation with his friend Gerald when the phone started to ring. Ed continued his conversation as if the phone hadn't rung. After a few rings it quit. Gerald asked him about this: "How come you didn't answer the phone?" Ed answered quietly, "I had the phone installed for my convenience. It wasn't convenient for me to answer the phone now."

People always object, "But what if it is an emergency?" My answer is that in thirty-plus years in the ministry, I guess I've been involved in a typical amount of emergencies, and they always seem to get through to me if it is important. I have been on vacation fifteen hundred miles from home, ten blocks from a phone, and in a rainstorm—and somehow, in a real emergency, someone managed to get through!

The point is simply this—quality uninterrupted times must be available to us to work on the things we feel are vital and strategic—whether they are prayer, study, ironing, planning, reading, rest, earning an M.B.A., or writing the great American novel.

THE DOOR

Another source of interruptions for the homemaker is interruptions from neighbors or salespeople or fundraisers knocking at the door. Each of these must be handled on an individual basis.

In some cases, you simply don't let them in—explaining that they called at an inconvenient time and you won't be able to spend time with them this morning. In other cases, you simply don't answer the door. You have that option; answering the door is *your* decision. To borrow from Ed Tom's philosophy about telephones, "You had the front door built (or bought a house with a front door) for your convenience, and right now it isn't convenient for you to open it."

Of course, if you choose to open your door selectively, it's a good idea to have a peephole installed so you can monitor your visitors. Such a peephole is a recommended safety device, especially when you are at home alone. (Be sure to check identification of any stranger who knocks before you let him or her in your house!)

THE FAMILY

Undoubtedly the greatest source of interruptions for the homemaker is her own family—spouse and children. This takes a great deal more thought, care, and sophistication to deal with.

We need to recognize that in the very choice of getting married and having children you have, as a matter of fact, opened your life up to the needs of others in ways that you cannot ignore. And, as Martin Mull has observed, "Having children is like having a bowling alley installed in your brain!"

If, on top of kids, you have chosen to have a career along with a family, you are indeed hostage to all of those previous decisions. Your family, like mine, has legitimate demands upon your time, energy, and resources.

The problem develops when patterns and expectations grow over a period of years so that time for yourself and your goals is squeezed out by the increasing demands of these significant others in your life. This is particularly true when children are small and almost totally dependent upon your attention, time, and energy.

Once again, what will work well for one person will not work well in another situation—but there are many possibilities.

A good friend of mine named Georgina Wells is a single divorced parent who has two children aged nine and thirteen. She works thirty-five hours a week as a counselor and has all the normal involvements of work, phone calls from clients, church activities, personal friendships, and hobbies in her life. She also likes to read and attend conferences about her vocation.

She has found that for her the best plan is to have a young nanny, a twenty-one-year-old girl from Sweden, to live and work in their home for room and board and some financial compensation. The girl also works part-time outside the home and takes some classes in the local junior college. They have developed a style and a schedule in which they all profit from the relationship.

Here are a few modest suggestions (from one who is admittedly limited in his ability to advise homemakers) for the mom (or dad) who finds herself (or himself) in the crunch of family demands:

Enlist Your Spouse. You do this by sharing with him or her your need for expertise and assistance in getting you more time to work on your important goals. Approach your mate as a potential ally in this matter as it may require more of his or her time and energy in sharing of parental or household responsibilities—as well as reprioritizing some items in the family budget (such as sending laundry out or hiring a once-a-week housekeeper). The key opening line is, "Dear, I need your help."

Enlist Your Children. One of the most easily committed omissions for most modern parents is the failure to enlist and train children in helping around the house—cooking, going to the store, even planning some of the meals.

Although I have admitted that I am not fully qualified to advise homemakers, I *am* qualified to speak on this particular subject. As I mentioned in an earlier chapter, when I was a teenager I was in virtual charge of the household needs for our family of three while my widowed mother worked. I did the house cleaning, shopping, washing, and ironing—and those were the days before automatic washers and dryers, when everything had to be wrung out and hung on a line.

In a way, I was a homemaker for five years. Granted, I didn't have any babies or toddlers to care for. But I was a kid, and I learned kids can do many helpful things to participate in the family work.

Anticipate and Adjust Your Attitude. Anticipate through your own knowledge and planning specific ways that you can structure your abilities to meet your family's needs more efficiently. Many problems can be solved by simply knowing how to restructure your time—and by readjusting your attitude. If you believe you are responsible to make it happen, if your family is a friendly resource to be recruited as co-conspirators, and if you believe it *can* happen—the likelihood is much stronger that it *will* happen!

One of the reasons I feel so strongly that it is possible for homemakers to be in charge of their lives so that they can accomplish high-level goals is that I have known those who have done it—and continue to do it. In fact, it never ceases to amaze me, as I have counseled with women over the past three decades, what varied mental attitudes homemakers bring to their tasks, and what a difference those attitudes make.

I have known some women who have all their housework chores done by nine in the morning! (Yes, they get up early, are well organized, and are decidedly compulsive.) We have one woman in our church who during the past ten years has managed to get her C.P.A. certification and her M. B. A. while also getting married and raising two children. She also worked for three years during this time as the head of the tax department of a large computer company, and now she has completed her first two years of law school. Admittedly, she is very bright. But more important, she is highly motivated and energetic and has recruited her husband and her mother as an ally.

On the other hand, I have known other homemakers who have no children and yet who always seem to be overwhelmed. They never seem to get anything done. The thing that becomes obvious after listening to a great variety of people's stories is that the number of children and even the age of the children and the external circumstances are not always the key. Invariably the decisive ingredient is the individual's attitude toward life itself.

A homemaker's greatest resource for getting time for herself and her high-priority goals is her ability to set up her unique screens—and this depends on her mental perspective. If she feels she is not in control, and it won't work—then it won't. If she assumes that she is in control and can do something, the odds are pretty good that she will make marked progress and begin to find time for whatever she deeply desires to attend to.

═══ SUMMARY ═══

Your attitude toward life is going to be more confident and affable when you have purged the time and energy wasters and you are regularly spending some systematic time on what you consider your highest and most satisfying goals. God has given you gifts and tasks and a portion of time to manage. You will feel better about the whole process of life when you know you are not wasting your life on a lot of nonproductive nonsense but are really making a difference.

Living Bodaciously 13

We have two worship services on Sunday mornings, and usually the second presentation of the sermon is the better of the two. One reason for this is the responses I get from people after the first service as I greet them at the door. Often they will give me an additional illustration or idea that I can use to enhance the sermon in the second service.

This is just what happened to me one Sunday, when I was preaching in the early service on the topic, "Designed to Win." My sermon stressed how to make "winning" happen in your life, trying to give some practical ideas for how people could make the coming week a winning week in their lives.

It was one of those overly ambitious seven-point sermons, and I really had to move it along to hit all the points. I touched on six practical steps a person should take, and then I arrived at the climax of the sermon—pulling out all the stops as I hit number seven: I encouraged the congregation to go out that week and tackle the week with a courageous spirit of action—to live boldly, courageously, and enthusiastically. And I closed with those powerful words of Tennyson's *Ulysses:* "To strive, to seek, to find, and not to yield."

It was a good sermon, and I felt good about it. After the 9:30 A.M. service, I went to the door to greet people—and one of our members, Marc Marcussen, came up to me with a smile on his face and a gleam in his eye. He stuck out his hand and said, "I've got the word for your last point—*bodacious*. You hit the nail on the head—we have to go out and live life *bodaciously!*"

And then Marc proceeded to share with me how his family had used this word they had gleaned from the famous "Snuffy Smith"

195

cartoon strip. *Bodacious!*—a word that beautifully combines the two elements of *boldness* and *audacity*. To live bodaciously, we need to attack life with *both* of these qualities.

And this is the theme I want to share with you in this chapter. A confident and affable life is rich for many reasons. And one of the most important is that it includes living with excitement, enthusiasm, and a sense of importance and zest; with a gladness of heart, with courage and vigor—living *bodaciously*.

The Bible is clearly supportive of the idea of facing life and the tasks of life with high courage, motivation, and desire. The apostle Paul said, "Whatever your task, work heartily, as serving the Lord and not men, knowing that from the Lord you will receive the inheritance as your reward; you are serving the Lord Christ" (Col. 3:23–24).

In several other places Paul talks about the intensity of his desire and motivation in serving Christ. In Colossians 1:29, he describes his intensity this way: "For this I toil, *striving with all the energy* which he mightily inspires within me" (emphasis mine).

And then, in the Book of Revelation, the church at Laodicea is severely criticized for her tepid attitude: "I know your works: you are neither cold nor hot. Would that you were cold or hot! So, because *you are lukewarm*, and neither cold nor hot, I will spew you out of my mouth" (Rev. 3:15–16, emphasis added).

It is in living bodaciously that we intentionally exercise several important dynamics of the abundant and satisfying life:

=== TAKE CONTROL ===

We can only be bodacious as we are in control of our lives. Being enthusiastic is not only a reminder that we are making decisions and taking control of our emotional attitude; it also helps keep us aware of the fact.

If a person protests that he doesn't *feel* all that enthusiastic, I would say that is probably the greatest reason why he needs to exercise his flaccid bodacity muscles—daily. My advice would be that he take his highest priority goal, tack it on the wall, and start out each morning reaffirming his commitment to move toward the goal that day with high motivation.

In being bodacious, we are zealously focusing in on the importance of what we are doing, focusing in on the fact that we have chosen to *take control* rather than merely be controlled by circumstances, by others, by the weather or the stock market.

This is a vital and strategic attitude because it is an antidote to that kind of pseudo-piety that enervates many Christians—the kind of piety that expresses itself by passivity, by floating, by limply slopping through life. Such a tepid faith is often defended as being "spiritual"—and its defenders will endlessly quote passages of scripture about how important it is to "wait upon the Lord," without striving "in the strength of the flesh."

And I would be the first to acknowledge when there are times when such counsel is appropriate, but not all the time.

I confess this passive attitude was once very attractive to me —mainly because it took a great deal of responsibility off of my back. (And I would still be the first to acknowledge that there are times when it *is* appropriate to wait on the Lord, leaving my circumstances completely up to him.) But then I started reading biblical passages such as Colossians 1:29, where Paul talks about "striving" and "energy."

That was a new thought! God has given us energy; he inspires that energy within us. And Paul says our responsibility is to strive to use that energy! That's bold and audacious in its view of life and accomplishment.

I keep thinking of a river. Many of us have lived by a river at one time or another in our lives. How fascinating they are—especially if they are big rivers navigated by great ships!

Picture in your mind such a large river. As you look at it, some things are moving upstream against the current, making waves, and other things are floating idly downstream—no waves at all. Did it occur to you that most of the things that are merely floating with the stream are dead, while the things that are moving against the current represent life? Living things may use the current as their ally, but they don't merely float. They go cross-current, they go upstream, they make waves. Dead things drift idly, passively, and don't disturb the water at all.

The bodacious life is not the life that merely floats like a dead fish downstream. No, the bodacious life is like the salmon in the rushing current—turned upstream, moving, darting, jumping, making things happen. As Oliver Wendell Holmes wrote, "To reach the port of success we must sail, sometimes with the wind and sometimes against it—but we must sail, not drift or lie at anchor."

Think of the stories of bodacious men and women in the Old Testament. Joshua leading the Hebrews into the Promised Land. David taking up the battle against Goliath. Deborah assembling the people of God against the Canaanites. Read Hebrews 11 and hear the roll call of the faithful:

> And what more shall I say? For time would fail me to tell of Gideon, Barak, Samson, Jephthah, of David and Samuel and the prophets—who through faith conquered kingdoms, enforced justice, received promises, stopped the mouths of lions, quenched raging fire, escaped the edge of the sword, won strength out of weakness, became mighty in war, put foreign armies to flight. Women received their dead by resurrection. Some were tortured, refusing to accept release, that they might rise again to a better life. Others suffered mocking and scourging, and even chains and imprisonment. They were stoned, they were sawn in two, they were killed with the sword; they went about in skins of sheep and goats, destitute, afflicted, ill-treated—of whom the world was not worthy—wandering over deserts and mountains, and in dens and caves of the earth (vv. 32–38).

One of the biblical stories that is most challenging to me in terms of bodacity is the story of the early church in the Book of the Acts. You find boldness on virtually every other page. The record says that they testified to the resurrection of Christ with *boldness*, and were thrown in jail because of it. Later they were released and were warned, "Don't speak any more in the name of Jesus." So what did they do? Acts says that they went back to their groups and prayed more fervently for *boldness* (Acts 4:29).

Take control and act boldly! Step out with preplanned, calculated boldness. Live bodaciously!

=== LIVE NOW ===

When and where are you living—in the past, in the future, or today? Rabbi Louis Binstock has written:

> Too many of us waste our years waiting for better times in the future or wondering about better times in the past, instead of working for better times in the present. If only we had lived in better times or had been born in better times! If only we lived with better people or belonged to a less underprivileged and despised group! If only we lived in a better home or a better town! If only we had a better business or a better job! If—
> If—
> If! Tomorrow—
> Tomorrow—

Tomorrow! But today is always there; yesterday is gone, and tomorrow may never come. No, now is the time—here is the place. This is the person. This is your home. This is your job. This is your wife—your husband—your child—your mother—your friend. This is your people. This is your country. This is your generation. You can have a wonderful time just where you are, just when you are, just how you are, just with whomever you are.*

It goes without saying that this statement of Rabbi Binstock must not be pushed to the extreme. But his point is well taken. Don't spend so much time and energy lamenting over what *might be* to the detriment of taking advantage of what *is*. Maximize today and your present circumstances.

Bodacious living is living to the fullest in the present, exploring, developing, and exploiting the many opportunities that are at hand; finding the acres of diamonds that Russell Conwell used to talk about in his famous speech (later made into a small book, *Acres of Diamonds*)—the diamonds that are right in your own back yard. As stockbroker Charles M. Schwaab has written, "The best place to succeed is where you are with what you have."

=== *GET ENTHUSED ABOUT YOUR WORK* ===

How does one get excited about one's work? First you must find work that fits your skills and talents—work that is important to you and to others.

William Feather wrote, "Work is dull only to those who take no pride in it." What kind of work could you really take pride in? Writing a sonnet? Carving a statue? Solving an engineering problem? Building a program? Stirring an audience? Designing a building? Cooking a terrific meal? There are as many answers as there are people.

Some years back, Norman Vincent Peale wrote a book entitled *Enthusiasm Makes the Difference*. I think he was right—especially where work is concerned. Your life at work can be lived on a level of dull and dreary endurance, painful duty, laborious languor—or it can be attacked with enthusiasm. Bodaciously!

*Quoted in *A Treasury of Success Unlimited*, ed. Og Mandino (New York: Pocket Books, 1984), p. 25.

GET A LITTLE FANATIC
ABOUT SOMETHING

Ralph Waldo Emerson once said, "There is no strong performance without a little fanaticism in the performer." I believe he had something there. When I look carefully at the people I consider to be successful in life, almost without exception there is something a bit excessive about some dimension in their life. Very close to their strength is also something that goes a bit overboard—or at least it would be considered overboard by those who are less successful!

Certainly this is true of many writers whose lives I have examined. Elton Trueblood, it is reported, is something of a fanatic on the use of his evenings. According to one account I heard, he places very specific limits upon committee meetings, and is likely to say something like this to a group: "Whatever we are going to accomplish tonight, I trust that we will be done by 9:45 P.M.— because that's when I am leaving." And he leaves at 9:45 P.M.— whether or not the meeting is finished.

Jonathan Edwards, the great Puritan divine, spoke of himself as "resolved to live with all my might, while I do live." I like that. As long as we are going to live—we might as well do it with a touch of excess.

The apostle Paul put this way, "Whatsoever you do, do it *heartily*, as unto the Lord and not as unto men."

And a parallel thought—if less elevated—is that proclaimed on TV beer commercials: "If you can't go with *gusto*—don't go at all."

ACCEPT YOUR LEVEL OF INTENSITY

One caveat must be noted here, however. Every one of us has our own unique level of intensity; we are not all designed to live in hyper-drive.

Various levels of bodacity and motivation are readily visible in the lives of people around us, and it is generally acknowledged that to excel in anything takes a good deal of drive and desire. For instance, Johnny Miller, the pro golfer, was quoted in the *Los Angeles Times* as saying,

> I don't know what happens to me. I guess I lose my desire. I could never be as good as Nicklaus. I guess I am not sufficiently motivated. I don't lie awake at night worrying about whether I win a lot of major championships. I couldn't care less. I am not a driver, not the way Gary Player is, Lee Trevino, Arnold Palmer, Hale Irwin

and even Nicklaus, who is really dedicated. I am more like Julius Boros or Gene Littler. I like to win but it's not life or death with me. I think it will help my longevity. Take a guy like Hubert Green. He's so intense; in 10 years he will be talking to the trees.*

Of course, what is not said here is that all people have to find their own level of motivation and desire—their own Bodacity Index—that works for them. Though Johnny Miller doesn't put himself in the same league with some of his more intense colleagues, his level of motivation works well for him, and he seems to feel it will keep him going for the long haul. Because we are each unique, the same level is not necessarily right for each person.

═══ STRIKE OUT COURAGEOUSLY ═══

The bodacious life is one in which people get excited about issues bigger than themselves and they throw themselves courageously into life's opportunities. That kind of life can be scary and it can be risky—as it was for Papillon—but it can also be thrilling and intensely fulfilling.

A couple of years ago, Pastor Doyal Van Geld shared the following story with me. I believe it epitomizes the kind of risky living we're talking about:

Picture a bleak battlefield scene—World War I, in France. Rows of trenches scar the landscape. On one side are the Germans, and on the other side are Americans, and separating them is a very narrow no man's land. The fire exchange has intensified; a young German soldier attempting to cross that no man's land has been shot and become entangled in the barbed wire. He whimpers in pain, and occasionally he cries out in agony.

Between the shells, all the Americans can hear him scream. When one American soldier could stand it no longer, he crawls on his stomach out of the American trenches and toward the wounded German. The Americans, realizing what he was doing, stop firing; the Germans continue until a German officer realizes what is going on. He stops his men from firing, and now there is a weird silence across the no man's land.

On his stomach, the American makes his way to the German soldier, disentangles him, then stands up with the German in his

*28 May 1976, "Morning Briefing" Part III, page 2.

arms. He walks straight to the German trenches and places the
wounded soldier in the waiting arms of his comrades, then turns
and starts back to the American trenches.

Suddenly a hand on his shoulder spins the young American
around. There stands a German officer wearing the Iron Cross, the
highest German honor for bravery. He jerks it from his own uni-
form and places it on the American, who walks back to his side.
When he is safely in the trenches, the war resumes.*

═══ FIND YOUR MOTIVATION ═══

What will it take to motivate you to move smartly toward a confident and affable relationship with life? Papillon stood on the cliff
and came to that crucial moment—to jump or not? And he
jumped. He was motivated to act bodaciously because he wanted
freedom so intensely.

Many are the people who have contemplated the principles set
forth in this book but have lacked the motivation to do anything
about them. This is one of the great mysteries of life—what will
ignite a woman or man into living boldly and powerfully? What
will quicken him or her into action?

You may have heard the wonderful old story of the young man
who decided to take a shortcut home through the large, dark
cemetery. As he crept through the graveyard, which he thought
he was familiar with, he fell into a deep open grave and found he
couldn't get up and out over the slippery sides. He was too far
away for anyone to hear him, so he finally realized he might just
as well settle down and go to sleep until morning. After a short
while, another fellow took the same shortcut through the cemetery and fell into the same open grave. As the second man was
thrashing about in the dark, trying to climb out, the first man
was awakened and said from the corner, "You can't get out of
here!" BUT HE DID!

So here you have two men in the same hole. One is motivated
to get out, and the other is stuck. What about you? Will you, like
Papillon, catch the super-waves that are all about you? These
things I have shared with you are tested and proven methods of
building a confident and affable relationship with life. If you
have the motivation, these principles can work for you.

*Printed in *The Pastor's Story File*, March 1986 (Saratoga, CA: Saratoga
Press) p. 1.

=== *SUMMARY* ===

Live boldly and courageously. Get hot or get cold, but don't stay lukewarm. Live heartily; be responsible for the control of your life. Strive mightily with all the energy Christ has put within you. Live now. Get enthused—even a bit fanatic about something; get intense. Life is too full of potential to be missed. Be courageous. Don't let handicaps hold back your spirit. Be bodacious!

Epilogue
A Hostile and Lovely World
Invites Your Response

We live in a hostile world. It is a world of sweat, pain, cancer, betrayal, bereavement, war, and tears. I am aware of these ugly realities. The admonitions of this book were not written from an ivory tower.

I know what it means to tow a busted car home more than two hundred miles on more than one occasion. I know what it's like to carry a full load in both college and seminary while working forty-eight hours a week and raising a family. I understand what it means to have a doctor give me bad news—cancer—and then insert obscene, painful pieces of hardware into several tender orifices of my body. I have had gall bladder surgery and radical prostate surgery (where they cut out everything but lust). I have had heart disease for almost ten years and have experienced obesity and arthritis. I have suffered disappointments and, on several occasions, the ill-effects of my own strategic bad choices.

I write as one who experienced the death of parents at an early age—my dad died on his forty-sixth birthday (when I was thirteen), and my mom died at age fifty-three (when I was twenty-two) after a two-year bout with cancer that wasted her life away.

I understand that we live in a real world in which our children can go through divorce. I have plumbed the depths of mediocrity, procrastination, bad choices, and wrong moves for myself. I have been visiting people in convalescent hospitals for three decades and have few illusions about that set of realities. I have had to speak at the funerals of a number of my closest friends. Believe me, I am no Pollyanna.

Yes, I understand that we live in a tough and hostile world. But I deeply believe that, even in this given hostile world, we can

204

learn to develop a confident and affable relationship with life—thanks to Jesus Christ.

As George Santayana wrote, we can become bitter or better. We can learn and share and give in the midst of the hostile world, or we can rant and rave and fulminate. We can gather companions along the way, or we can gather enemies. We can find the ways to life that were pioneered by Jesus Christ, or we can merely suffer and, to quote Dylan Thomas, "Rage, rage against the dying of the light." Our philosophy can be "Life is mean and dirty—and then you die," or it can be "For to me to live is Christ, and to die is gain" (Phil. 1:21).

Papillon stood on the edge of a cliff. Behind him was imprisonment, in front of him the pounding, forbidding surf. He focused on freedom and escape, and he turned his back on being a prisoner.

How a person chooses to respond to the hostile world before us all is the choice each one of us has been given. I pray that for you it will be to lay hold of the confident and affable attitude toward life that is available to us in Jesus Christ. Read the New Testament through carefully, prayerfully. Ask God to show you the truths he has there for you.

It is true that we live in a hostile world. But it is also a world of buttercups and peach blossoms, loyal and loving friends, shimmering seas, vast panoramic vistas, euphoric feelings, promising adventures, and exciting prospects. Even when the skies are dark, it has meteor showers and lightning bolts and the promise of a new day's dawning.

Which data do we chose to focus on and affirm? Which world do we seek to extend? Which world do we think represents the eternal plan? We are invited to choose. And we can get a start by choosing God's affability principle—which is to put on the Spirit and love of Jesus Christ. As Paul points out in Colossians 3:12–17,

> Put on then, as God's chosen ones, holy and beloved, compassion, kindness, lowliness, meekness, and patience, forbearing one another and, if one has a complaint against another, forgiving each other; as the Lord has forgiven you, so you also must forgive. And above all these put on love, which binds everything together in perfect harmony. And let the peace of Christ rule in your hearts, to which indeed you were called in the one body. And be thankful. Let the word of Christ dwell in you richly, as you teach and admonish one another in all wisdom, and as you sing psalms and hymns and spiritual songs with thankfulness in your hearts to God. And whatever you do, in word or deed, do everything in

the name of the Lord Jesus, giving thanks to God the Father through him.

══ A BRIEF REVIEW ══

In summary, what we've tried to say is that we need not enter life like a sailor taking to uncharted waters. Many have made the journey before us and have noted the shoals, the channels, the haunts of Scylla and Charybdis and the Great White Shark. The sacred Scriptures underline and clarify these principles for us. And people of wisdom and understanding in virtually every civilization and culture have found these keys and passed them on.

WINNERS AND LOSERS

There is a continental divide that separates people—a dividing line. On one side of the line are those who observe and have the courage to use the forces God has put in nature. On the other side are the timorous who hold back and remain prisoners to their fears and their doubts; their frustrations, impotence, and bad habits.

God has good plans for each of us. He wants us to experience his best intentions—which is life abundant. As God told the children of Israel through Jeremiah: "For I know the plans I have for you, says the Lord, plans for welfare and not for evil, to give you a future and a hope" (Jer. 29:11).

AFFABILITY

God intended for each one of us to be uniquely prosperous and affable winners who succeed in life.

Affability is a specific combination of virtues that combines patience with people, kindness, joy, and a peaceful disposition. This constellation of attitudes is very close to what Paul describes in Galatians 5:23 as the fruit of the spirit: "But the fruit of the Spirit is love, joy, peace, patience, kindness, goodness, faithfulness, gentleness, self-control." A word that sums up several of these virtues is *affable*.

Affability is to human relationships what graphite is to a lock or oil to an engine. It makes relationships work better, with less friction. To be affable is to get along with people. It is my firm conviction that as we follow these clear, tested, and biblical principles we will develop a more affable relationship with life itself.

UNIQUENESS

God built amazing and dramatic specialty into the animal world. Examine the patterns of animal life, from insects to whales, and you find incredible diversity. So also, God made each one of us unique. In all the incredible billions of years that the astronomers say they can compute, there has only been one of you. Cherish the incredible opportunity of your singular life. As you discover the great value of your particular identity and mission, you will be able to relate to people with a much more confident and affable demeanor.

ABUNDANCE

God wants you to experience abundance in your life. In a particular sense, God wants you to be rich. Jesus said, "I come that they may have life, and have it *abundantly*" (John 10:10, emphasis mine).

God's Word teaches that each of us is to be rich in his or her own special way. We each have a special set of gifts and opportunities. The sooner we find out precisely where our prospects for unique richness are located, the more confident and affable our lives can become.

CLARIFICATION

One of the greatest enemies of a truly satisfying life is fuzziness. Many people are not really sure who they are, where they are going, what is important to them, or who is important to them. Their lives are confused because there are many forces in our culture that continually muddy the waters.

A confident and affable life is more possible when you have a clear view of who and what is important to you. You need to cut the fuzz and settle in on who you are and where you are going.

GOALS

A goal is a future state or event that you seek to accomplish. It can be measured in time and by performance standards. Goals should be clear, not fuzzy. They should be written in pencil, reviewed regularly, and modified. They should be positive, authentic, and designed for a specific time period (short-term, intermediate, or long-range). They should be big enough to make you stretch without being unrealistic.

A PLAN

The affable life doesn't just happen. It is carefully planned—like catching Lisette at just the right moment with a bundle of coconuts in hand.

A plan begins with processing your high priority goals. Out of this process will emerge further clarification and a better idea of how to go about reaching your goals.

OBLIGATIONS

To live an affable life—in the best sense of the word—is to be obligated—not obligated with the stifling, draining proliferation of competing and mindless obligations exemplified so richly in the fallen, pagan world about us; not obligated in a slavery to sin that oppresses; but, like Paul, obligated by an overarching compulsion to obey Christ and to be open, authentic, giving, and loving. To be properly obligated is to love even in and through our weaknesses, brokenness, and vulnerability.

MINDSET

We can set our mental "filter" to include or exclude, diminish or highlight selected kinds of input from the world around us. We can filter life in such a way as to enhance it and focus on the beauty and colorful variety of life—and thus make it more affable. Or we can filter life so as to see only dolorous shades of gray and black. We adjust our "filter" by setting our minds, and the Bible says we are responsible for the way our minds are set. We can set them on the kingdom or on the chaos. We can tune them to: (1) search for and discover life's hidden treasures; (2) taste life fully and experience it enthusiastically; (3) focus on belonging; or (4) focus on triumph and victory in Christ.

What will be the spirit of your lifelong mindset? It is for you to choose whether you will rust and atrophy—or shine with use.

CONTENTMENT

One mindset choice is between contentment and discontent. Some choose discontent in the midst of a life of power. Paul chose contentment while in jail. We live in a world that only knows how to count wealth and resources in one way—by the dollar—but true contentment comes from things that cannot be calibrated in dollars.

PURGE THE NONSENSE

You can live a more successful life if you purge out the wasteful nonsense—those things that devour your time, your energy, your focus, your attention, and that detract from your accomplishing the things you believe are truly important. It is an inelegant fact that many simply dissipate their lives on things that don't even matter to them, much less to anyone else.

BODACIOUS

Live boldly and courageously! Get hot or get cold, but don't stay lukewarm. Live heartily, be responsible for the control of your life. Strive mightily with all the energy Christ has put within you. Live now. Get enthused—get a bit fanatic about something; get intense. Life is too full of potential to be missed. Be courageous, motivated, and bodacious.

HOSTILE AND GLORIOUS

We live in a hostile world. It is a world of sweat, pain, cancer, betrayal, bereavement, war, and tears. In a sense it is like Devil's Island—surrounded by threatening, pounding surf. But it can also be a launching platform for the beginning of high spiritual adventure, if it is the place that you begin to discover escape and freedom as provided in Jesus Christ.

═ MY COMMITMENT ═

Now that I have read *How to Live Confidently in a Hostile World*, I covenant before God to begin working daily and systematically on the following goals:

_____

_____

_____

_____   _____

Signature   **Date**